The Myths and Truths of Lean Transformations

How to Successfully Make the Transition from Theory to Effective Deployment

T0293292

The Myths and Truths of Lean Transformations

How to Successfully Make the Transition from Theory to Effective Deployment

By
Raymond Kelly

A PRODUCTIVITY PRESS BOOK

First edition published in 2019
by Routledge/Productivity Press
711 Third Avenue New York, NY 10017, USA
2 Park Square, Milton Park, Abingdon, Oxon OX14 4RN, UK

© 2019 by Raymond Kelly
Routledge/Productivity Press is an imprint of Taylor & Francis Group, an Informa business

No claim to original U.S. Government works
Printed on acid-free paper

International Standard Book Number-13: 978-1-138-29638-1 (Paperback)
International Standard Book Number-13: 978-1-138-29639-8 (Hardback)
International Standard Book Number-13: 978-1-315-10006-7 (eBook)

Library of Congress Cataloging-in-Publication Data

Names: Kelly, Raymond, 1952- author.
Title: The myths and truths of lean transformations : how to successfully make the transition from theory to effective deployment / Raymond Kelly.
Description: New York : Taylor & Francis, [2019] | Includes bibliographical references and index.
Identifiers: LCCN 2018020478 (print) | LCCN 2018034176 (ebook) | ISBN 9781315100067 (e-Book) | ISBN 9781138296381 (pbk. : alk. paper) | ISBN 9781138296398 (hardback : alk. paper)
Subjects: LCSH: Organizational effectiveness. | Quality control.
Classification: LCC HD58.9 (ebook) | LCC HD58.9 .K434 2019 (print) | DDC 658.4/013--dc23
LC record available at https://lccn.loc.gov/2018020478

**Visit the Taylor & Francis Web site at
http://www.taylorandfrancis.com**

Contents

About the Author

Raymond (Ray) Kelly is the proud recipient of a BS in Engineering Operations from North Carolina State University.

Ray is a seasoned Lean Six Sigma practitioner with over 25 years' experience as a hands-on industry practitioner holding senior management positions in the USA and Asia. His manufacturing employers have been Eaton Corporation (automotive), Telex Terminal Communications (computer peripherals), Northern Telecom (telecommunications), Cardinal Health (medical devices), and Littelfuse (electronics components). Ray first became involved in just-in-time (Lean) manufacturing in the early 1980s and holds several patents for pioneering work in developing manufacturing processes.

Additionally, Ray has over 15 years of experience in management consultancy whilst developing subject matter expertise in Lean manufacturing, Six Sigma deployment and supply chain optimization. He has been employed by several of the big consultancy firms; Coopers & Lybrand, PricewaterhouseCoopers, and Deloitte Consultancy. He's also owned a consultancy business and worked as a freelance consultant. Ray has provided consultancy expertise to an extensive and diversified range of clients in more than 20 countries. His client list includes Hewlett-Packard, Texas Instruments, Manitowoc / Frymaster, Abbott Laboratories, Panasonic, Toshiba, Suzuki, Siemens, Infineon Technologies, Unilever, Mead–Johnson Nutrition, Royal Dutch Shell, and British Petroleum.

Ray is a certified Lean Six Sigma Master Black Belt.

Ray has a passion for leading companies in substantial business transformation initiatives. He has led over 100 initiatives, resulting in annualized cost savings of over $200 million.

Some of the quantitative results that Ray has successfully facilitated include:

- 40~67% reduction overall process lead time;
- 35~90% reduction in cycle times;
- 33~65% reduction in raw material inventories;
- 25~70% reduction in finished goods inventories;
- 50~72% reduction in work-in-process inventories;
- 24~50% reduction in late deliveries;
- 30~50% reduction in labor hours/unit;
- 20~58% reduction in scrap rates;
- 25~71% reduction in customer complaints;
- 30~60% reduction in floor space;
- 60~80% improvement in overall quality;
- 30~97% reduction in set-ups/changeovers.

The case-in-point examples (over 60) in this book reflect Ray's hands-on experience leading Lean Transformation initiatives. He is very proud of his accomplishments in the deployment of Lean Six Sigma Tools and methodologies within a very diversified business landscape. The goal of this book is to share his successes, as well as a couple of failures, with you.

Introduction

Been There, Done That ...

...now, let me share my experiences and, hopefully, make your Lean journey less turbulent.

I am writing this book as I want to share my real-life experience as a Lean Implementer. I hope that I can inspire some of you to relentlessly pursue operational perfection within your organizations, and at the same time take some of the apprehension away by showing you that while the deployment of Lean has substantial underlying scientific and mathematical merit that a lot of success can come from common sense applications. I've heard it said many times that Lean is a combination of science and art; that's very true, but a good dose of common sense and humility doesn't hurt, either. Although, you can be an expert in the deployment and application of Lean tools and methodologies; you'll be most successful by engaging and respecting all levels of your organization. And, also, exhibiting humility is beneficial to each of us; I have over 40 years of operational experience, but I am a lifelong learner and always try to keep an open mind and learn from everyone that I encounter (sometimes learning what not to do ☺).

I probably have as diversified a Lean background as anyone. I have been an engineer, a manager, a director, a consultant, an entrepreneur, and a CEO / president. I have led more than 100 Lean / Lean Six Sigma projects in 23 countries. I have been employed by American Fortune 1000 companies; and have consulted American and foreign multinationals, and national & regional companies alike.

The projects that I have led have resulted in annualized savings of greater than $200 million, while training and mentoring over a thousand participants in Lean tools and methodologies.

I am a certified Enterprise Lean Six Sigma Master Black Belt and have coached, mentored, and trained hundreds of Yellow, Green, and Black Belt practitioners.

So, it should be somewhat obvious that I've ... been there, done that ... so now it's time to write about it and share my experiences (good and bad).

I'm hoping that you'll find some inspiration and gain some valuable knowledge from a seasoned Lean Practitioner. I think and hope that my passion for Lean (a.k.a. Operational Excellence) will become very obvious. So, as I started to write this book, I felt the need to turn it into a how-to book based on my own experiences (case stories).

Lean and Common sense

I always think of Lean as being in large part common sense, but I also know that common sense has different meanings and is perceived very differently by many. So, what I perceive as being common sense may not be perceived in the same way by others. Therefore, I have collected a few notable quotes regarding the significance of common sense.

The first quote, below, is probably my favorite and actually sums up a lot of why I'm doing this book i,e, make the transition from the theory of Lean & Continuous Improvement to practical, common sense practices .....

> *Common sense is something that you already know ... once someone points it out to you.*
>
> **Ron Mascitelli***
> *(author of Mastering Lean Product Development:*
> *A Practical, Event-Driven Process for*
> *Maximizing Speed, Profits and Quality)*

I'm hoping that my case-in-point examples will point out the common sense aspects of Lean that registers in a common sense way with you, also.

I have included some other common sense quotes that I hope provoke some Lean analogies for you.

---

* Mascitelli, R. *Mastering Lean Product Development: A Practical, Event-Driven Process for Maximizing Speed, Profits and Quality.* Northridge, CA: Technology Perspectives, 2011.

This one, below, is very relevant to achieving a successful Lean Transformation:

The three great essentials to achieve anything worthwhile are: Hard work, Stick-to-itiveness, and Common sense.

Thomas A. Edison

As is this one …

Common sense is seeing things as they are; and doing things as they ought to be.

Harriet Beecher Stowe

Others …

Common sense is genius dressed in its working clothes.

Ralph Waldo Emerson

Common sense is not so common.

Voltaire

Common sense ain't common.

Will Rogers

Application of common sense is Intelligence.

Ramana Pemmaraju

Common sense is instinct. Enough of it is genius.

George Bernard Shaw

I hope this helps you understand my perspective on the synergy of Lean and common sense.

Chapter 1

Enterprise Lean Transformation Introduction

Lean Transformations: Creating & Maximizing Customer Value

So, what is a "transformation"? Generically, a transformation is thorough or dramatic change in the form or appearance of an item.

Therefore, an Enterprise Lean Transformation is the end-the-end transformation of a company's order fulfillment process: i.e. a Lean Transformation of the order fulfillment process would maximize customer value while minimizing waste throughout the process and sub-processes (Figure 1.1).

The objective of a holistic Enterprise Lean Transformation is the alignment of an enterprise's focus (or purpose), processes, and resources across all value streams to maximize customer value while minimizing waste across the enterprise.

A transformation's ultimate goal must be to maximize customer value;

so, how do we define value from the customers' perspective. (Figure 1.2)

Creating and maximizing value for the customer means:

- raising quality levels – zero defects, Six Sigma;
- raising delivery and service levels – 100% on-time-in-full (OTIF), 100% supply reliability, transparent collaborating;
- reducing costs: win–win cost reduction sharing, managing supply chain inventory and cost;
- reducing response time – shortening process lead time, shortening overall order fulfillment times, shortening replenishment times.

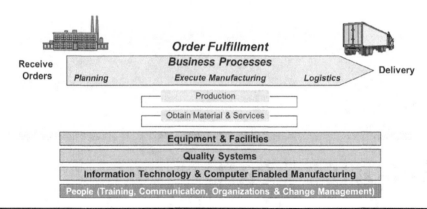

Figure 1.1 A simple representation of a typical enterprise's order fulfillment and support processes.

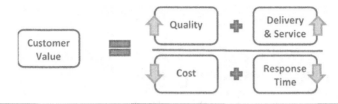

Figure 1.2 Creating value for the customer.

However, we must continuously verify how our customer defines value (more definitive breakdown of the above four core values); we should always validate the Voice of Customer (value definition from the mouths of our customers and direct feedback on our performance). This will be my first reference to the "boots on the ground" approach; we need be talking directly with our customers as we need to be a presence for them.

So, the *focus* of the Lean Transformation should be to *provide maximum value to the customer through perfect processes that consist of zero waste.*

And how do we define "waste"? *Waste is the utilization of any more than the minimum amount of resources required to deliver the desired value to the customer (internal or external).* I'll discuss "waste" in more detail later in this book.

A Lean Culture Transformation changes the focus from the optimization of segregated activities, technologies, assets, and vertically structured functional departments (i.e. departmental silos) to the optimization of the flow of products and/or services through value streams that flow horizontally to customers across activities, technologies, assets, and departments (Figure 1.3).

To transform your business, the focus should be on the processes, not the individual functions, as a value stream is no more than a series of related processes that deliver a product or a service. The best way to ensure that

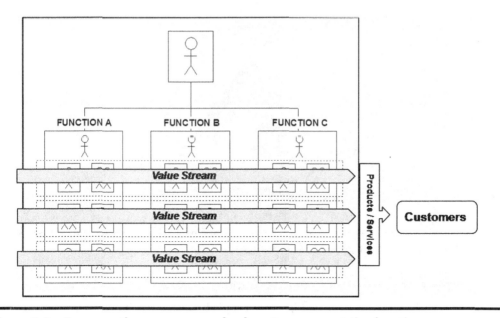

Figure 1.3   Focus on the processes and value stream … not the functions.

you deliver a quality product or service is to control the process, and the first step in the Lean Transformation is to identify and remove inefficiencies (a.k.a. waste) from the process (and organization). Eliminating waste throughout the value streams, instead of at isolated activities, creates processes that require fewer operators and assets and less space and time to make products, or that enable the delivery of services at far lower costs and with far fewer defects compared with traditional business thinking. Lean Transformed companies are more responsive to changing customer desires and are of higher quality, lower cost, and shorter throughput times. In addition, information management becomes simpler and more accurate.

In a business transformation initiative, it's imperative that there's clear accountability and ownership for all processes during the transformation. Through all phases of the transformation (planning, assessment and execution), you must engage upstream and downstream stakeholders to get a balanced perspective.

Change Readiness, i.e. Appetite for Change

One of the real challenges of any enterprise or business transformation is determining the organization's appetite for change. Every organization has to decide if their goal is incremental changes, or if they are willing to seek breakthrough changes: i.e. changes that will modify their competitive

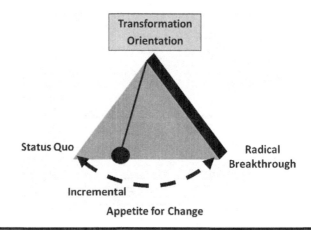

Figure 1.4 What's your appetite for change?.

landscape. Many organizations may settle for somewhere in between status-quo and radical-change, but aligning your organization's goals with the organization's appetite for change is critical to the success of your transformational journey. Every transformation must be a journey with a clearly defined end goal. And that goal must align with your enterprise's appetite for change (status quo or breakthrough) (Figure 1.4).

Case-in-Point Example 1.1 Appetite for Change FAIL

I hope it's not bad omen to start off my book with a failed case-in-point example, but I think it's important to understand that if a company is not prepared to make and accept the necessary changes, then failure is imminent. During my consultancy days, I had a chance to visit a Southeast Asian semiconductor manufacturer and make a proposal to address a burning platform. The burning platform in this case story was excessive inventory at all levels: raw, WIP, and finished. I personally created the proposal knowing that I had addressed all of the concerns of the company's CEO. After our consultancy firm was awarded the consultancy contract, I met often with the CEO, and he made it clear that the inventory issue was keeping him awake at night. My role on the project was Project Management Oversight and Subject Matter Expert (I was supporting multiple projects in multiple countries). As my team started the assessment, it became very apparent that the CEO's staff didn't share his perspective that the company's inventory situation was an urgent burning platform. They strongly felt that the current inventory levels were required to satisfy customer requirements. So, there was a definitive disconnect between the CEO and his staff. The CEO was seeking monumental breakthrough changes, while most of his staff was OK with status quo or incremental changes at the most. I had a very seasoned Project Manager onsite and our team did a good job in their assessment; and under my guidance, we had a very good action plan to meet the CEO's targets. But we never proceeded to implement any of the proposed changes; the company's staff pushed back hard on all proposed changes. The CEO held me personally responsible for this failure, as he thought that I should have been able to convince his team of the benefits of the breakthrough changes. Unfortunately, I couldn't even get his team to agree to a proof-of-concept pilot runs in order to validate the benefit of the proposed changes: the CEO's team united to totally disrupt any and all proposals. They had zero appetite for change, even though the CEO was starving for it. And this CEO would never tell his staff that they must change; he had empowered them. The CEO passionately believed that my team was responsible for successfully selling the changes to his staff. As a side note, I was terribly handicapped on this project as the CEO's staff spoke minimal English; as a typical "old" American, I spoke only one language. Anyway, the moral of the story is that if a team is resistant to change and doesn't see the urgency in the need for it, then they will not change. This was one situation in which being a consultant was a hindrance, as I was not part of their team. Companies will often bring in consultants to overcome their staff's resistance to change by leveraging the consultant's expertise and diversified experiences but in this case, the company's staff resistance to change overcame the common sense & financial aspects of changing. So, the key is for a company to really gauge the appetite for change across the enterprise and align their transformation initiative accordingly.

Some keys to overcoming resistance to change include:

- ■ #1 – communicate:
  - two-way communication;
  - communicate the burning platform and sense of urgency;
  - WIIFM (what's in it for me), etc.: show them data.
- ■ communicate clear goals and a roadmap to success. Engage everyone on the journey;
- ■ gain some buy-in (traction) upfront with some quick wins;
- ■ link transformation targets to change in bonuses, compensation, etc.

What Comprises an Enterprise Lean Transformation Model?

The Enterprise Lean Transformation Model addresses the three key elements of a transformation, focus, processes, and resources (Figure 1.5).

At the top (a.k.a. roof) of the Transformation Model is Focus (a.k.a. Enterprise Focus).

- ■ *Enterprise focus*: The focus of a Lean Transformation should be simple and obvious; i.e. the maximization of customer value while utilizing the minimum amount of resources possible. As part of defining your appetite for change, you'll need to define the scope of your transformation initiative. For example:

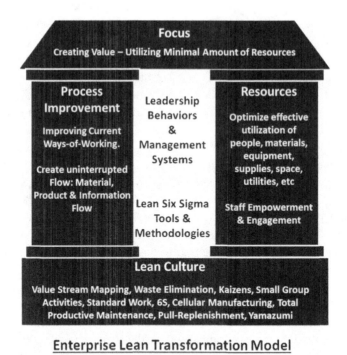

Figure 1.5   The Lean Transformation Model.

- Should you include suppliers, and if so, which ones? (think vital few vs. trivial many);
- Should you include customers, and if so, which ones? (think vital few vs. trivial many);
- What part of your product portfolio should be included in the scope of the process?

The support (a.k.a. pillars) for the transformation are the Processes (operational & administrative) and the Resources (e.g. people, infrastructure, material, etc.).

■ *Process*: The process goal of your transformation should be improving the order fulfillment (and supporting) processes for the creation of uninterrupted "flow", i.e. the continuous flow of material, product, and information throughout the order fulfillment process. And "flow" is best realized by the elimination of "waste". "Waste" will be thoroughly discussed in Chapter 2.

■ *Resources*: The transformational goal for an enterprise's resources has been previously stated: minimal resources while producing maximum customer value. Resources include people, materials, equipment, supplies, space, and utilities. Optimization of resources can be obtained by:
  - elimination or minimization of wastes: i.e. muda, muri, and mura (see Chapter 2),

- developing the capability of people throughout an organization, and
- empowering and engaging staff.

The element which connects the Processes with the Resources is the Leadership & the System.

■ Leadership Behaviors and Management Systems

With processes and resources as the pillars of our transformation model, the key enablers of our transformation effort will be leadership, management systems, and the effective deployment of Lean and Six Sigma tools and methodologies across the enterprise.

- *Lean Leadership Behaviors include:*
  - Being customer-focused and understanding that whatever you and the organization do should be aligned with creating maximum value for the customer.
  - Going to the Gemba is one of the best tools that a Lean Leader has: i.e. go to the source and get the facts. I assume that most of you are familiar with the term Gemba. As I have been told and have read countless times, Gemba is a Japanese word that translates into the "real place" or "real thing"; so, I'll just accept that that as a true translation and/or definition of Gemba. For the most successful Lean Leaders, this tool becomes a behavior. And it's a behavior that should be a strong component of their Leaders Standard Work (more on Leaders Standard Work later).

Here's a very interesting quote from Taiichi Ohno on leadership and going to the Gemba:

> *When you go out into the workplace, you should be looking for things that you can do for your people there. You've got no business in the workplace if you're just there to be there. You've got to be looking for changes you can make for the benefit of the people who are working there.*

- Facilitating effective problem solving: It seems to be human nature to cut our problem solving activities short; i.e. to jump to conclusions as to the root cause. And that's why we are often solving the same problem multiple times, because we failed to identify the root cause(s). Lean Leaders should drive the consensus of the immediate process stakeholders of the root causes; they should reinforce the use of a systematic methodology such as PDCA, DMAIC, 8D, etc. Conclusions must be fact-based, data-driven, and data-validated. Problem solving is not a situation for opinions based on assumptions.

Going to the Gemba is an effective component of a robust problem solving initiative. If there's a problem, go to the place where the problem is occurring, confirm the facts and analyze the situation, and make a decision accordingly. Then initiate any containment or countermeasures that may be required.

• Walk the continuous improvement talk. I'm sure that you've been told many times that if something isn't broken, don't try to fix it. The Lean Leader must ignore that thinking; a Lean Leader must lead continuous improvement, be proactive, fix things before they break, and change things just to get incremental improvements. To a Lean Leader, the status quo is unacceptable.

• Lean Leaders should be process-oriented; control the processes and you'll ensure the quality and performance of the product(s). And in all instances, Lean Leaders must demand fact-based, data-driven solutions. There is a quote credited to Dr. Joseph Juran that I love; he supposedly held up a one-dollar bill to a group of students, showing them the inscription "In God We Trust". To paraphrase, he told the group: "In God, I trust; everybody else bring me data". That should be the mantra of Lean Leaders: show me the data. A combination of facts, data, and Gemba-verification will produce the most robust solutions to any issue.

– *Lean Management System*

Lean Leadership is a main component of a Lean Management System, which is the infrastructure that promotes continuous improvement through the deployment of Lean tools and methodologies. It nurtures the engagement of all associates while striving to maximize value to all customers (internal and external).

Besides Lean Leaderships, other key components of a Lean Management System include:

• Hoshin Kanri: Lean strategic planning and development
  ■ Hoshin Kanri is a strategic planning and developing approach that has been widely accepted by the Lean community. Hoshin Kanri is a systematic process for aligning, communicating, and executing business strategy by focusing on those vital few breakthrough objectives. Breakthrough objectives are goals that can only be achieved through significant changes to the way the company operates at all levels. A company cannot achieve these objectives by continuing business at the status quo.

■ Hoshin Kanri is a disciplined method for ensuring that the strategic goals of a company drive progress and action at every level of the enterprise. It achieves this by aligning the enterprise's breakthrough goals (the What, with a 3~5-year horizon) with the plans of next-level leadership (the How Far, with a 2~4-year horizon) and the annual priorities (the How and How Much, with a 1~2-year horizon but focusing mainly on next 12 months).

The goal of the Hoshin Kanri approach is to:
  – establish a clear linkage between strategy and execution;
  – align business functions and activities to overall strategic goals;
  – create a medium to communicate clear sense of direction;
  – provide a guide to achieve strategic objective through specific plans with clear owner and timelines.

The mechanism that Hoshin Kanri utilizes to achieve this alignment (strategy with execution) is the "X-Matrix". An X-Matrix is a one-page document that shows an organization's strategic plan of breakthrough objectives and then cascades this down to the next level, then the next level, and so on.

Figure 1.6 is an example of an X-Matrix.

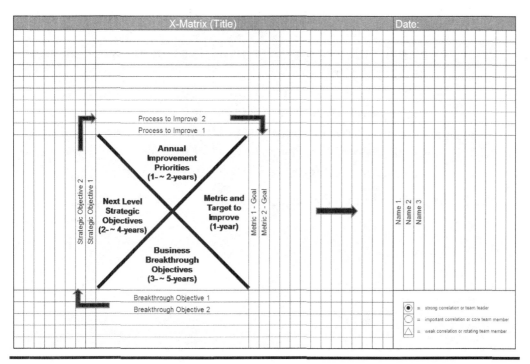

Figure 1.6   Example of a standard X-Matrix format.

The steps to complete an X-Matrix are:

- Step 1: Input X-Matrix title (company or function) and date.
- Step 2: *What*: Add breakthrough objectives (3~5-year horizon). Highest priority is closest to the center. Breakthrough objectives are goals that can only be achieved with significant changes (i.e. an enterprise transformation) to the way the company operates at all levels.
  - Is it a breakthrough objective?
  - Is it a measurable, stretch goal?
  - Is it linked to customers' expectations, i.e. the Voice of Customer?
  - Will it provide a significant competitive advantage?
- Step 3: *How Far*: Add next-level strategic objectives (2~4-year horizon). Highest priority is closest to the center.
- Step 4: Correlate the breakthrough objectives with the strategic objectives (strong, important, or weak correlation).
- Step 5: *How*: List annual improvement priorities (1~2-year horizon). Highest priority is closest to the center.
- Step 6: Correlate strategic objectives and annual improvement priorities (strong, important, or weak correlation).
- Step 7: *How Much*: Add metrics and targets to improve. Targets to be obtained within one year.
- Step 8: Correlate annual improvement priorities and metrics and targets to improve.
- Step 9: *Who*: Add resource allocations and accountability (i.e. team leader, core team member, or rotating team member).
- Step 10: Correlate metrics and targets to improve and the breakthrough objectives.

The steps are highlighted on the X-Matrix in Figure 1.7.

The X-Matrix should be cascaded across all levels of the enterprise (Figure 1.8).

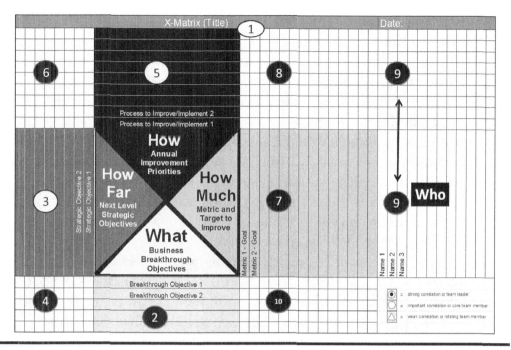

Figure 1.7   Steps for completing an X-Matrix.

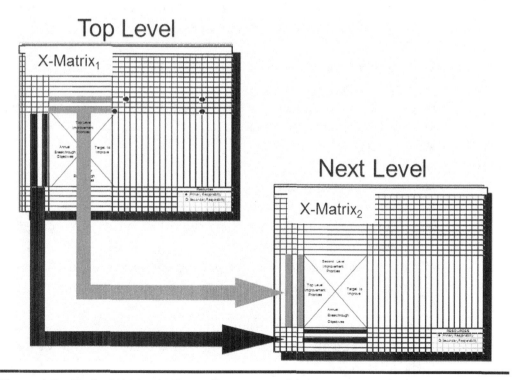

Figure 1.8   Typical X-Matrix Cascading (rotate objectives counter-clockwise).

Metrics (True North)

The utilization of key performance metrics is a crucial element of the Lean Management System, as it's an often repeated statement that you can't improve what you don't measure. Transformation progress is quantified by improvement in performance metrics. True North is a vision of the ideal condition, and it challenges status quo thinking. It's the ideal state (think VSM) that you want your organization to strive for. True North is often seen as your guide for doing what your organization should do, not what you can do.

True North is the compass point for your Lean Transformation, your guide from getting from point A to point B, where "A" is your current state and "B" your ideal state.

True North metrics provide guidelines for the enterprise in achieving its goal (or achieving True North). It's a measurement of your enterprise's improvement. True North metrics can be aligned in four categories: safety/respect for people, quality, delivery, and cost.

Here are some examples of True North metrics:

- Safety/respect for people
  - safety performance: e.g. lost time, first aid instances;
  - participation/engagement: e.g. number of kaizen events, training attended, certification levels, etc.
- Quality
  - customer-based metrics: e.g. complaints, returns, satisfaction indexes, etc.;
  - process performance: e.g. yields, scrap, rework, variances, etc.;
  - supplier quality/performance;
  - total cost of quality.
- Delivery
  - process lead time (PLT);
  - manufacturing cycle time;
  - customer fill rate/on-time delivery/perfect order percentage/ on-time-in-full (OTIF)
  - new product development: e.g. time-to-market, development process lead times, engineering change orders/notices, etc.
- Cost
  - productivity; manufacturing cost;
  - total manufacturing cost (excluding materials) per unit or per headcount;
  - total cost of ownership;

        ■ inventory turns;

        ■ cash-to-cash cycle time.

– Engagement. Employment engagement at all levels is an important element of development of a Lean Culture and an integral part of a Lean Management System.

– Standard Work (a.k.a. Standardized Work) is the backbone of the Lean Management System. Standard Work documents the best way to perform a task or activity. Standard Work must be established for production associates, technicians, etc. and all levels of leadership. There is further discussion on this in later chapters.

– Visual Management

    Visual Management entails managing your business via visual controls and, perhaps most importantly, being able to identify any abnormalities at a moment's glance (≤ 30 seconds).

    Visual Management is achieved by organizing, in plain view, all tools, materials, production activities, and production system performance indicators so that the status of the system can be understood at a glance by everyone involved. This is often referred to the "30-second rule": i.e. anyone should be able to come into an area and, within 30 seconds, determine the operational and performance status of the area. (Note: There are many variances to the 30-second rule, such as the 10-second or 20-second rule. Regardless of the time, the key is "at a glance".)

    Communication boards should be able to answer these simple questions in 30 seconds or less:

    • What is the purpose?

    • Who is it for?

    • How often do you use and/or respond to indications of abnormality? What are the escalation steps?

– Accountability

    Accountability is a key ingredient of a Lean Management System and flows from the top down and the bottom up. Everyone must hold themselves accountable for their personal actions as well as for the actions of their teams. Peer-to-peer accountability falls into the respect for people category. I personally think that any company will struggle to create a successful and sustainable Lean Culture if this ingredient is lacking.

Being accountable means not only being responsible for something but also, ultimately, being answerable for your actions. It is something you hold a person to only after a task is or is not done.

■ Lean Six Sigma Tools and Methodologies

There is a fairly extensive array of Lean Six Sigma Tools and Methodologies that will be deployed throughout an Enterprise Lean Transformation, starting with the assessment stage and culminating with defining new ways of working. Throughout this book, I'll discuss many Lean Six Sigma Tools and Methodologies, starting with the assessment stage of a transformation "how-to" below.

■ Lean Culture

So, the *Sustaining* foundation of your transformation will be the adoption of a Lean Culture by your organization.

The best way to sum up the anti-Lean Culture is, I think, is conveyed by the old saying (proverb) that you have probably heard many times before: "If it ain't broke, don't fix it". This basically means that if something is working reasonably well, or is reasonably successful, then there is no need to change or replace it.

Well … that's the opposite of a Lean Culture.

The philosophy of a Lean Culture is to proactively make it better, deliver it faster, and/or produce it cheaper.

So, if "If it ain't broke, don't fix it" is your current paradigm, then Lean requires a paradigm shift. You must continuously strive for improvement, even if nothing is broken – if you don't, then you risk losing your customers.

Always strive for "Better, faster, cheaper", as the status quo is unacceptable in a competitive landscape.

I'll discuss the components of a Lean Culture as we proceed through this book.

Case-in-Point Example 1.2 Lean Management System

I have been lucky in that I have worked with over 60 companies, which has exposed me to some of the best and worst Lean Management Systems. The worst systems are typically seen in companies that boast about what great Lean/Six Sigma initiatives they plan to undertake – but then they never accomplish anything. These companies typically have very strong verbal "leadership". They talk a great talk but don't seem to understand the importance of being "seen" rather than "heard". The companies that fail at Lean/Six Sigma are typically brought down by resistance to change on the part of their leadership. It was easy for them to verbalize support for change but not so easy to physically or mentally embrace changing their business. And these leaders, typically, will spend loads of money: hiring consultants, paying for training, investing in launching improvement initiatives, etc. But when it comes down to accepting and implementing improvement initiatives, they don't have the stomach for anything larger than incremental (insignificant) changes. They usually go for surface-coating initiatives such as 5S, which they will haphazardly implement without ever gaining any actual benefit. But 5S posters will proliferate on the walls of their facilities. A Lean Management System will not succeed unless a company's leadership is willing to make a commitment to substantial changes in their current ways of doing business.

Before I move on to sharing some best-in-class Lean Management System deployments, I wanted to mention one observation that I've made over the years. Lean and Lean Management System can succeed without undying commitment from senior management. I have been involved in many very successful Lean Transformations in which senior leadership was not the flag-bearer of Lean and/or Lean Transformations. But they take the leap of faith and empower some key subordinates, and those subordinates' subordinates, to embark on and embrace a Lean Transformation journey. And they'll give enough positive lip-service to the transformation initiative to allow it to gain the traction needed to be successful. Actually, I think this is the scenario that is prevalent and successful in most companies. Leadership (CxOs, presidents, etc.) has enough confidence in their subordinates to empower them to lead any transformation of their business; they'll just monitor the performance scorecard.

Now for some personal testimonials of best-in-class Lean Management System deployments.

Case-in-Point 1.3 Building a Lean Culture

I want to share some insight into two global companies (industry leaders in their fields) that I had first-hand opportunities to be an integral part of their Lean Management Systems: they both leveraged Lean (a.k.a. Operational Excellence) as a competitive advantage. Key ingredients of both systems included their training and people development schemes, coupled with great engagement campaigns – and both systems showed great respect for their employees.

Both companies' Lean Management Systems had the full support of the senior management/leadership team, including the CEO. And both had senior leadership steering committees that drove global strategies and policies and that sought input from the global manufacturing sites. The leadership at both companies definitely walked the talk when it came to continuous improvement and the establishment of strong, sustainable Lean Culture.

Although the training format and curriculum varied significantly between the two companies, both had very structured curriculums and reward/recognition schemes. They also both embedded continuous improvement in the DNA of their associates. The status quo was to always be challenged, and taking calculated risks was rewarded, not punished. One of the companies gave its employees a "License to Hunt": i.e. to go find waste and eliminate it.

One of the companies promoted employee engagement through the deployment of Small Group Activities (SGAs). SGAs ... think Quality Circles. And I must say that that was the most effective engagement scheme I have ever witnessed. Each manufacturing cell had its own "natural" cohesive cross-functional group that was empowered to make changes within their cells with minimal management intervention. They exhibited great pride in their cells and the accomplishments of their groups. These groups were comprised of engineers, technicians, and operators. The site, at which I resided, had organized competition sessions every 4~6 weeks, which varied by theme, rotating between safety, quality, delivery, and cost. This overall scheme gets a production associate engagement rate of greater than 85%, which I would consider world class. These SGAs were linked to tiered meetings; the SGAs had daily standup meetings in their area at their communication boards to discuss their performance in safety, quality, delivery, and cost, along with issues that were within their control. These were considered Tier 1 meetings; their immediate management would hold Tier 2 meetings covering a broader scope. The site management would have Tier 3 meetings, and so on.

The Healthcare Service company had an annual global competition for best kaizens, Lean Projects, and Six Sigma Green Belt and Black Belt projects. This was a very prestigious and competitive competition. The requirements for entry into this competition were strict, but the competition received hundreds of entries each year from around the world. The competition was open to manufacturing, supply chain, and administrative personnel.

Case-in-Point Example 1.4 Building a Lean Culture Part 2

Another success story that I'd like to share is a US OEM manufacturer of industrial equipment. I had little actual involvement in the implementation of this system, but I participated in its successful deployment. This company had vertical four-sided rectangle communication boards located at most production lines, fabrication areas, etc. Every morning, the Director of Operational Excellence would lead a Gemba Walk through a timed route to many (almost all) of the communication ("Managing Daily Improvement") boards. The Director of Operational Excellence's Gemba Walk core team was small – Production Area Manager/Plant Manager/Site Director, Quality, and Materials – and this roaming team would be met at various boards by the area process owners (production supervisor, Lean engineer/technician, quality rep (if not with core team). These boards were set up in tradition fashion to cover SQDC (safety, quality, delivery, cost), with each "Assembly" area board including a simple but effective hour-by-hour board.

This daily end-to-end Gemba Walk took about one hour but was very effective. They didn't try to solve any problems during the walk, but actions were assigned as needed. There was definite assigned accountability and urgency for all assigned actions: this company's leadership team held people accountable, and there was strong peer-to-peer accountability. Respect for people (others) was embedded in the DNA of the company and all its staff. The company had issues, but they worked vertically–horizontally in a collaborative approach to address them.

How to Get Started with Your Enterprise Lean Transformation Initiative?

At the start of a transformation initiative, you must complete an assessment of the business's current ways of working and identify improvement opportunities. The assessment should create a gap analysis of the current ways of working versus industry best practices utilizing a data-driven, fact-based assessment approach in alignment with industry bet-practice databases and a set of proven tools and methodologies (Figure 1.9).

The comprehensive assessment would include an external and internal assessment.

The "external" assessment would look at several factors:

- Voice of Customers (VoC): The VoC is a process to understand the expectations of your external customers: i.e. how your customers define "value". VoC allows us to define what is critical to quality (CTQ) from the customer's perspective.
- Competitor Landscape: A competitor landscape allows you to differentiate your strengths and weaknesses from your competitors' strengths and weaknesses. It is a great area to utilize a SWOT diagram to identify your competitive strengths, weaknesses, opportunities and competitive treats.
- Supply Landscape: A supply landscape is an assessment of your enterprise's supply management strategy, including suppliers' geographic alignment, lead times, inventory levels, quality and delivery performance, and manufacturing/supply chain capabilities.

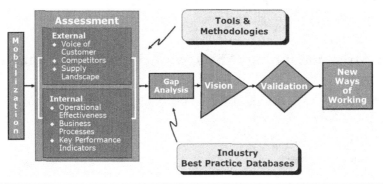

Figure 1.9 Assessment framework.

The "internal" assessment establishes a baseline of the enterprise's current ways of working and its performance.

Key elements of the assessment are:

- Operational Effectiveness
  - material, product, and information flow;
  - value stream process lead times (PLT);
  - value-added vs. non–value-added ratios;
  - facility layout effectiveness (distances traveled);
  - quality performance (yields, scrap, rework, cost of quality, etc.);
  - productivity.
- Business Processes
  - overall effectiveness of your current ways of working;
  - hand-offs;
  - approvals;
  - value stream process lead times (PLT);
  - value-added vs. non–value-added ratios.
- Key Performance Indicators (KPIs)
  - order fulfillment: order fulfillment lead time, frozen order periods, customer responsiveness, cash-to-cash cycle time;
  - inventory: days of inventory (DOI), turns, work in process;
  - delivery: on-time-in-full (OTIF);
  - overall equipment effectiveness (OEE).

There are several tools and methodologies that can be used to complete the internal assessment, but my preferences are:

- **Routing By Walking Around (RBWA), with the following analytical elements:**
  - value-added vs. non–value-added activity segmentation;
  - number of operational (or transactional) steps;
  - spaghetti diagram (distance traveled);
  - hand-offs.
- **Value Stream Mapping (VSM), with the following analytical elements:**
  - value-added vs. non–value-added activity segmentation;
  - identify seven wastes;
  - process lead time (PLT);
  - inventory levels;

- bottleneck(s)/constraints;
- quality and quality gates.
■ **Process Mapping** (swim-lanes)
- a swim-lane allows mapping a process across various departments, functional groups, etc.
■ **Triple Play Chart: Production vs. Demand vs. Inventory**
- a Triple Play chart compares your production output versus the actual customer demand versus your inventory level.
■ **Overall Equipment Effectiveness; Performance, Availability, and Quality**
- changeover times;
- total productive maintenance (TPM);
- preventative/autonomous maintenance.
■ **Yamazumi** (operator balancing and productivity)
- a Yamazumi chart is useful tool to analyze the various elements of an operator's task or activities.
■ **Cost/Spend Analysis**
- an analysis of operating costs and spend to identify opportunities for savings.
■ **Cost of Quality**
- cost of quality looks at the cost to maintain good quality; and the negative costs associated with poor quality.
■ **A-B-C Analysis**
- differentiate the critical items verses the less critical; opportunity to establish different execution strategies, etc.
■ **Basic Quality Tools** (Pareto, histogram, run-charts, fishbone, control charts, etc.)

Both the internal and external assessments should follow the Pareto principle (a.k.a. 80–20 rule), which basically means that the assessment should focus on the vital-few rather the trivial many. This can also be defined through the T-Approach (Figure 1.10).

Case-in-Point Example 1.5 Results of a Lean Transformation

This case story is about a Japanese white-goods (household appliances) manufacturing site in Southeast Asia. The company was facing very strong cost-competition from many Chinese appliance manufacturers. So, we were contracted as consultants to lead a Lean Transformation to improve their overall competitiveness.

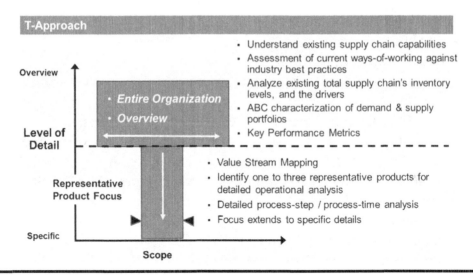

Figure 1.10 T-approach for drilling-down.

I led the initial steps of the project, which encompassed a full assessment of their current ways of doing business. This was a complex, vertically integrated facility with fragmented manufacturing departments (warehousing, metal-fabrication, plastic-molding, electronics, etc.) spread out throughout the site.

After the full assessment was completed and the performance gaps validated, the client prioritized the initiatives that they wanted to undertake as Phase 1 of their transformation journey and contracted our consulting services to assist them.

I led Phase 1 of the transformation, which included the following initiatives:

- Process flow modeling: Identify and minimize non–value-added activities. Redesigned several manufacturing cells, improving material and product flow at the shop floor.
- Implemented robust process controls (statistical and visual) and quality improvements initiatives, led an "attack" to identify and validate root causes of yield and scrap issues, and established process controls (poke-yoke) to prevent defects at the source.
- Machine set-up time improvement (SMED): Introduced parallel activities while machine is running and initiated some fixture and equipment design changes to reduce set-up time and increase production flexibility.
- Manufacturing run strategy: Categorized the product groups to create a manufacturing build schedule of daily and weekly buckets and optimized equipment and cell changeovers.
- Bottleneck optimization: identified bottleneck operation and optimized loading sequencing of products to meet demand.

- Capacity and line balancing and resource allocation: Allocated products to machines and cells to optimize the balancing of operational capacity per demand (Takt Rate).
- Kanban implementation: Implemented kanbans to control inventory and synchronize production to actual demand. Implemented supermarkets to decouple the fragmented functional departments.

The results obtained were:

- set-up time reduction of 97%;
- improved labor cost per unit by 20%;
- increased production capacity by 60%;
- annualized overtime reduction of US$200k in savings.

There were another two phases on transformation activities, which the company took on with the use of a full-time consulting team, but we did provide ongoing advisory assistance whenever requested.

The ending results was that the company survived the onslaught of Chinese competition and stabilized their market share.

Case-in-Point Example 1.6 Using a Lean Expert or a Lean Consultant

When undertaking a Lean Transformation, companies typically have to decide whether to engage a consultant or expert to assist them along their journey. I will share my point of view on this matter.

Personally, I have 40 years of operational experience, with about 15 years as a consultant; my experience includes working with three of the original Big 6 Consulting Firms, managing my own business, and working as a freelancer or contractor when the occasion arose. I have worked with literally hundreds of consulting colleagues, and there's definitely been a mixture of very good and extremely bad.

In my opinion, if you're seeking some help with your Lean Transformation (and I would strongly recommend it), then make sure that any potential consultants have practical hands-on operational experience, not solely as a consultant, in an industry-practitioner role. You want someone who's "been there and done that" at an accountability level: someone who has had to live with the transformation changes and make them sustainable after the "newness" has worn off.

Figure 1.11 shows a slide that I have previously utilized to promote my consulting business; it highlights some of the advantages of utilizing a consultant.

I personally have been involved with or led over 100 projects, most of which were substantial Lean Transformations initiatives. The projects have resulted in over $200 million in annualized savings.

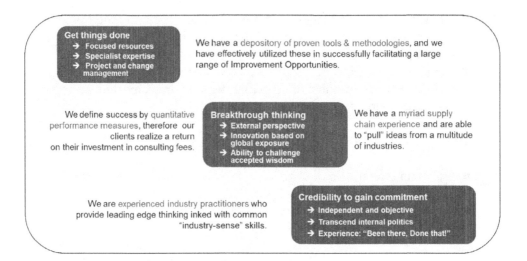

Figure 1.11   Potential advantages of engaging a consultant.

My consulting colleagues and I have typically obtained results such as:

- 40~67% reduction in overall process lead time;
- 35~90% reduction in cycle times;
- 33~65% reduction in raw material inventories;
- 25~70% reduction in finished goods inventories;
- 50~72% reduction in work-in-process inventories;
- 24~50% reduction in late deliveries;
- 30~50% reduction in labor hours/unit;
- 20~58% reduction in scrap rates;
- 25~71% reduction in customer complaints;
- 30~60% reduction in floor space;
- 60~80% improvement in overall quality;
- 30~97% reduction in set-ups/changeovers.

You'll quickly get a positive return on investing in consulting services if you wisely choose the right consultants to partner with your team. You want someone that can serve as a catalyst in your transformation journey: someone that can lead your team's transformation from ELSS common sense into ELSS common practice.

Assessment Tools and Methodologies

There is a large toolbox of tools and methodologies (as previously mentioned and described) that can assist you in creating the baseline for your Lean Transformation journey. I will provide you with some further information and how-to advice on utilizing some of the most commonly used tools and methodologies (at least the ones that I most commonly use).

Routing By Walking Around (RBWA)

One of the very first tools that I learned about as I was starting my consultancy career was Routing By Walking Around (RBWA). It's actual a very simple methodology, but it can be very powerful for analyzing the flow of a product through a facility.

I would highly recommend conducting a RBWA of a product before commencing a Value Stream Mapping (VSM) session for that product.

The RBWA is more detailed and will definitely help you uncover the "secrets" that exist.

An alternative approach would be to conduct your RBWA after using a "Current State" VSM session as a method to validate the information on the VSM. Either way, the RBWA and the VSM are complementary methodologies.

A RBWA is a tool that is easily defined by its name – Routing By Walking Around: it's the documenting of the flow of a single unit of product through a facility (or facilities) by physically walking the process as if you are the product (Figure 1.12).

To conduct a RBWA:

■ Pick a representative product to be the focus of your RBWA, remembering that you'll probably also be constructing a Value Stream Map for the same product. I usually choose a higher runner (Pareto's 80/20 rule) so that any improvements will have the largest impact on the bottom-line financials. It's always nice to show senior management/leadership a quick return on their investment in transforming their business.
■ After you have identified which product you'll be simulating through your RBWA, the next step is to identify which component (normally a raw material) of the product will be your starting point. You'll want

Figure 1.12 Routing By Walking Around (RBWA) analysis form.

to choose a key "base" material that is representative of the flow of the other components of the product. If possible, it should be the very first piece of raw material that is used to start the manufacturing of the product. This is definitely not brain-surgery, as they say, so just pick a representative raw material and go with it.

■ The starting point of your RBWA should be incoming/receiving (or at a minimum, the raw material warehouse).

■ To start the RBWA, start documenting each and every step (or activity).
  – List the steps in sequential order.
  – For each step, record how much time is required to complete task.
  – Take note of any inventory preceding or following each step (i.e. work in process). Record how much time it will take to typically process the inventory. *Note:* The RBWA is a snapshot in time, so record the inventory as it is when you are there; later, you can adjust based on inventory reports, etc. But for your RBWA activity, record exactly what you see on your walk around. Document the snapshot in time exactly as you witnessed during your RBWA. And be honest. You're not trying to find fault; you're trying to identify opportunities for improvement.
  – Record any distance that the "base" material travels through the process: i.e. travel accomplished by human (walking), fork-trucks, conveyors, automatic-guided vehicles, etc. You can also add the distance that the operator travels to get a tool, paperwork, etc. while the "base" is in the operators' workspace. Capture all travel distance of the base material and operators. Later, we can use this data/information to construct a spaghetti diagram.

■ After all the data has been captured, you'll want to perform an "Analysis of Time". The "Analysis of Time" is the classification of the various time-buckets, such as:
  – Value-added (VA) steps are the steps (activities) that the customer would be willing to pay; i.e. they're seen by the customer as adding value to the product. Value-added steps are often defined as any activity that changes the form, fit or function of the product. Depending on the industry, the value-added content of a current state process would seldom exceed 5%. And on the RBWA template, this time-classification is color-coded green as good (value added).
    • *Internal inspection*: A value-added step that may be open to debate is whether internal inspection is value added or not. Internal inspection is defined as the inspection of your own

work. Some folks will say any type of inspection is non–value added, as your process should produce perfect product every time. But I take a different view. No process is perfect; there are always variations. My perspective is that if you incorporate inspection into your handling of the part and ensure that no defects are passed on to your customer, then significant value has been created. On the RBWA template, this time-classification is color-coded green as good (VA).

 – The next set of time-classifications are all non–value-added (NVA) activities, and they are considered pure waste. These types of time are color-coded red on the analysis template. During your improvement activities, you'll want to eliminate or minimize these time-steps. The steps are:

  • *External inspection*: This is any inspection or testing of someone else's work. It's non–value added, as this is a downstream activity trying to identify defective product produced upstream. External inspection is trying to prevent defects from being passed further downstream; especially trying to ensure that defects don't reach external customers.

  • *Wait/Queue*: This represents a disruption in the flow of the product, so it's definitely non–value adding.

  • *Transport material*: Any transporting (movement) of material or product is classified as non–value adding.

  • *Motion*: Motion is the movement (handling) of a product, material, etc. by an operator or machine during the product transformation process. Motion is movement within the workstation or work area, not the transporting of material, etc. to/from workstations, areas, etc.

  • *Storage/Inventory*: Within most processes, the inventory within the processes is referred to as work in process (WIP) or raw in process (RIP). "Raw" refers to raw material stored in the production line and can also be used to classify subassemblies etc. stored within the production. WIP is limited to the product being produced, not its components. The focus is (should be) mostly on the WIP, as the amount of WIP directly affects the process lead time (PLT): i.e. Little's Law. Little's Law is represented by the equation: PLT = WIP / Exit Rate. Exit Rate is the number of units existing in the production area: i.e. the rate that product is completed and sent to the subsequent operations area.

– The final classification (color-coded yellow) is the non–value-added (NVA) activities that are waste but are required to enable the manufacturing of a product or the delivery of a service. They are non–value added but needed (NVAN). Examples include monitoring process chemicals (pH, viscosity, etc.) and regulatory testing or reporting. Within a manufacturing environment, there's very little that falls into this category. A litmus test to determine whether an activity is pure NVA or NVAN is, does technology exist that could eliminate, automate, replace, or make obsolete this activity? If the answer is remotely "Yes", then it's pure waste; if the answer is "No", then you may have justification for classifying it as NVAN. But regardless of whether it's NVA or NVAN, both should be treated as "waste" and seen as an opportunity for improvement.

Case-in-Point Example 1.7 RBWA

One of my most successful deployments of the RBWA analysis tool was for a Fortune 50 integrated semiconductor manufacturer. I was a consultant, specifically the Lead Consultant/Team Lead for Operations. The consultancy firm that employed me had been brought in by this company's Global President of Operations to do a full assessment of their order fulfillment process. This was a division of a huge American conglomerate; although our scope was limited to their Semiconductor Division, it still covered more than ten manufacturing sites in four countries. The main focus of my team's activities, however, was on their two-semiconductor assembly and test operations in SE Asia.

We used the "T" approach, through which we would get basic information on the full manufacturing portfolio and then "drill" down on a couple products. My initial RBWA would be constructed for a high-volume semiconductor device used by the leading mobile phone manufacturer (at that time).

This was only the second or third time that I had conducted a RBWA analysis – but no problem, I just jumped in. The first step is always to contact the person in charge to communicate to everyone along the device's processes that we would be performing an assessment of the manufacturing process flow of the designated device, but that we were not assessing any people. In addition, I needed a "guide", typically a senior manufacturing or industrial engineering type (but anyone knowledgeable of the process would suffice). With these things settled, I was ready to commence the RBWA.

No, I was not ready! I identified the device that I would be assessing but I hadn't identified the component that I wanted to "attach" to. I needed to break down the device and identify a component that I could follow from the incoming receiving process until shipping to customer. We often refer to this as "attaching" ourselves to a component, as we want to follow the component through every step of the process. For this device, the component that we chose to follow was the semiconductor wafer.

The starting point for my RBWA was the incoming material receiving area. So, from this point on, we wanted to "attach" ourselves to the wafer and follow it through the process. And as we followed it through the process, we recorded:

- Description of activity transformation and/or movement of the "wafer" (or the wafers' by-product, i.e. a die). Note: Break down the activities into work elements but mainly split into major value-added vs. non–value-added elements.
- The amount of time to complete the activity/work element. This is not a detailed time study, but we want to capture a reasonable estimate of how much time it takes to complete the tasks.
- The amount of inventory at the workstations or inventory buffers between workstations. The inventory to be counted is work in process only, not raw materials or offline built subassemblies. Important notes: (1) We are tracking the wafer and/or its by-product, so offline, etc. subassemblies are not counted. (2) This is a snapshot in time, So, we count (estimate) how much inventory (WIP) is present at the time of our RBWA. (3) The amount of inventory should be recorded as amount of time (days, hours, minutes, or seconds) required to process the inventory.
- The distance traveled by the wafer/die and travel distance by the operator required to transform the wafer/die into a product. For this particular case story, there was no extracurricular travel by the operator So, my distance traveled was limited to the travel of the wafer/die.
- The final RBWA step is to complete the "Analysis of Time": the classification of time as value-added or non–value-added activities/elements.

The results of this RBWA were:

- **Analysis of the Number of Process Steps**

    This process consisted of 178 steps (activities or work elements). Of these, 11% were classified as value added; thus, 89% were non–value added. The two largest categories of non–value-added activities (steps) were Delays/Queues and Transport (Figure 1.13).
- **Analysis of Cycle Time**

    The process total cycle time (a.k.a. process lead time (PLT)) is 342 hours. The amount of value-added time is 1%. The driver of the non–value-added cycle time differs from the driver of non–value-added steps. Of the total cycle time, 85% is devoted to storage (a.k.a. inventory), while 11% is non–value-added but required to move the product through the process (Figure 1.14).

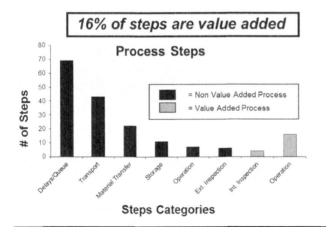

Figure 1.13 A visual example: Current state – RBWA process steps analysis.

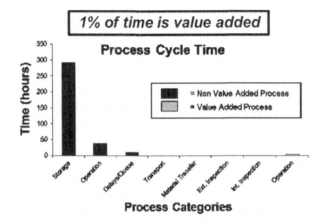

Figure 1.14 A visual example: Current state – RBWA cycle time analysis.

■ **Analysis of Distance Traveled:**

   The distance traveled was approximately 2,000 feet. To visualize the distance traveled, we constructed a spaghetti diagram (Figure 1.15). But this spaghetti diagram actually comprises a total of three products, which further show the congestion within the area.

Case-in-Point Example 1.8 Spaghetti Diagram

We can derive the following from the spaghetti diagram seen in Figure 1.15.

   ■ The layout followed a traditional manufacturing layout: i.e. similar equipment performing similar functions are grouped together (a.k.a. a farm layout, i.e. plant the same vegetables in the same area or row). The layout has product with crisscrossing flows, as it was laid out based on the function of the equipment, not the flow of a product or family of products.

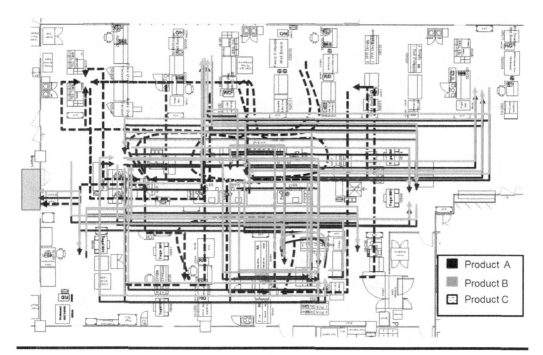

Figure 1.15   Example of a complex spaghetti diagram.

A potential humorous analogy (depending on your audience) of a scenario such as shown above: Due to large batch sizes, a single wafer would be within the manufacturing area for approximately 30-hours. So it would take a wafer 30-hours to travel 2,000 feet which is equivalent to 66.7-feet/hour which equates to about 0.01-miles/hour. And given that your typical garden variety snail moves at about 0.029-miles/hour; a snail is about 3-times faster than a wafer moving through this manufacturing process.

Figure 1.16   A humorous analogy.

■ The distance traveled (~2,000 feet) combined with 24% of all steps being transport; again, this reflects a poor layout. Additionally, the large amount of time I which the product is stored or queued (88% of total cycle time) reflects poor flow (Figure 1.16).

In summary, the RBWA is one tool to establish a baseline of current process metrics and identify opportunities for improvement. The visual examples shown above are nice ways to create a storyboard of the current state (as is) and show the impact of potential improvement opportunities – the future state (to be).

Value Stream Mapping

Value Stream Mapping is the mapping of the flow of material, product, and information through each value stream. The goal is to promote uninterrupted flow throughout the value stream, from suppliers to the external customers. Uninterrupted flow is achieved by minimizing work in process, minimizing waiting and queues, utilizing Visual Management to minimize the physical flow of information, and striving for one-piece product flow.

The steps for constructing a Value Stream Map assessment are as follows:

- Create a SIPOC chart (Supplier–Input–Process–Output–Customer), which:
  - ensures the correct stakeholders are involved in the Value Stream Mapping process
- Determine product and/or process family to Value Stream Map (VSM) and:
  - determine Takt Time
- Create the Process Flow Map using:
  - post-it notes or
  - whiteboard or brown (butcher) paper
- Add the material flow to the process flow map, including:
  - inventory, which is designated by a triangle of the Value Stream Map. I just recently learned two ways of calculating the amount of inventory within the value stream.
    - *Technique #1*: This technique can be extracted from the supposed VSM "bible" by Mike Rother and John Shook, *Learning to See*; it is the first book that I read on the subject of Value Stream Mapping. In *Learning to See*, the amount of inventory (WIP) stated on the VSM is determined by the equivalent process lead time (PLT). It is calculated as shown in Figure 1.17.

      The fallacy of this technique, in my opinion, is that there is no relationship with the consumption rate at the subsequent station. If the WIP is 10,000 pieces and the daily demand is 1,000

Figure 1.17 Process lead time calculation based on takt rate.

pieces, the PLT is 10 days, and so the inventory denoted on the VSM would be 10 days. The assumption is that the inventory will be used up in 10 days. I contend that this approach produces an inflated value for lead time and is not a true reflection of the VSM's current state.

- *Technique #2*: This calculation of PLT is based on Little's Law; to me, this technique is more realistic and more reflective of the VSM's current state. Here the lead time is calculated as seen in Figure 1.18.

  Using the same example above, if the WIP is 10,000 and cycle time at the station is 60 seconds, the lead time is 600,000 seconds or 10,000 minutes. Assuming a two-shift operation (21.5 hours), there would be approximately 1,290 minutes in a day, and thus the PLT would equate to approximately 7.8 days (10,000 / 1,290). The PLT is thus calculated based on the consumption rate (i.e. subsequent operations' throughput (exit) rate).

  I strongly support Technique #2, and when I train or coach others on VSMs, that is the technique that I use.

■ Add the information flow to the process flow map
■ Add and populate the process data boxes
- A tip here: don't be afraid of ranges to the data; it doesn't have to be a finite number. You should convey the variability that exists in the current process. Showing the variability in an activity is important for generating discussions about the nature of the variability and potential countermeasures to reduce it.
- The purpose of a current state map is to depict what is actually happening, so if variability occurs, it should be represented on the map.
■ Calculate the key VSM metrics: value-added ratio and process lead time (PLT)
■ Validate current state map via Gemba Walk
- A crucial part of the validating of the current state is to "go see the process". Go to the process and watch the operator perform the task: see what the operators are doing.
- Validate the current state map with as many stakeholders (upstream and downstream) as possible who were not a part of the VSM team. Get as many perspectives as you can. Engagement beyond the immediate team is important to ensure greater commitment to the successful implementation of the future state. The VSM team not sufficiently involving others (outside the VSM sessions) in establishing the current state is a common cause for failed future state implementations.

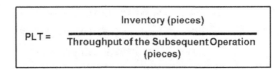

Figure 1.18   Process lead time calculation based on little's law.

■ Brainstorm "unconstrained" improvement opportunities (initiatives) for
the current state:
  – identify opportunities not constrained by money or existing
    technologies;
  – create a B&E chart (benefit vs. effort);
  – prioritize initiatives (management buy-in);
  – identify initiatives to be completed within the next 12 months;
  – create a Gannt chart for implementation initiatives ≤12 months
    (a.k.a. future state VSM).
■ Create "ideal" state Value Stream Map incorporating (kaizen bursts) all
  reasonable improvement initiatives (i.e. all initiatives BUT the bottom
  right area of B&E). The "ideal" state is the starting point for backward
  planning: i.e. what shall be included in future state rounds 1, 2, 3 ...
  (Figures 1.18 through 1.25).

Case-in-Point Example 1.9 VSM

One of my first applications of Value Stream Mapping was as a consultant
for an oil and gas company's upstream operations.

I had just arrived on the client's site the night before, and I wanted to
learn more about their process. There's no better or faster methodology
for understanding a process than to Value Stream Map that process with a
team of the client's subject matter experts (SMEs). The client had already
established a problem to be solved: i.e. reducing the cycle time from well
completion to pumping oil.

After the customary introductions, we immediately chose a large, blank
wall and started mapping the process utilizing post-it notes. Post-it notes
quickly proved to be the right medium, as there was considerable debate
among the SMEs as to the exact sequence of activities, particularly for
parallel concurrent activities. These debates, within a full range of SME and
upstream and downstream stakeholders, are very important in order to gar-
ner everyone's perspective. As the collaborative team proceeded through the
VS mapping process, we captured all information discrepancies/challenges,
issues, improvement thoughts, barriers, etc. in a "parking lot" flip-chart for
later investigations, validations, and/or discussions.

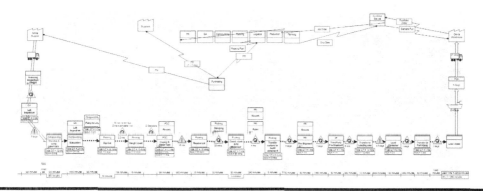

Figure 1.19   Current state value stream map.

Value Stream Mapping will drive
transformation initiatives..

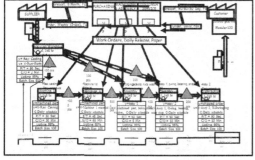

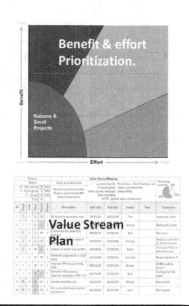

Figure 1.20   Value stream map + benefit and effort + value stream project plan.

		Benefit				Effort				
Project Selection Criteria and Significance Ratings	Cost Savings Impact 5 = $100k, 7 = $250k 10 =	Direct Links to Strategic Goals	Relates to Business / Process Objectives, e.g. Plant Goals	Customer Satisfaction impact / Improved Quality	Overall Benefit	Requires External Approval	Risk to Quality and/or Customer	Implementation Timeline 1 = ≤6-months, 5 = ≤9-months	Cost to Implement	Overall Effort
Potential Projects and Impact Rating										
Significance Ratings	10	10	10	10		10	10	8	8	
Scoring : 10 = Very High, 1 = Low										
Project	Savings									
1						$0				0
2						$0				0
3						$0				0
4						$0				0
5						$0				0

Figure 1.21   Example of benefit and effort development template.

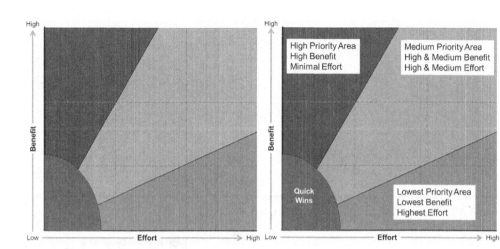

Figure 1.22 Visual representation of a benefit and effort analysis.

Project Status			Facility :				Updated:		Percentage Complete	

Figure 1.23 Value stream map project tracker (example).

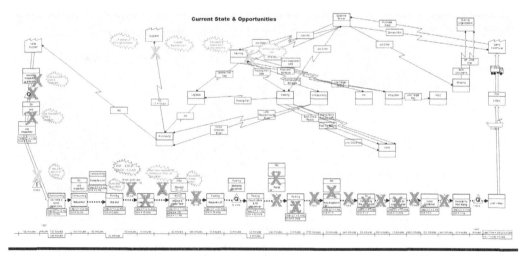

Figure 1.24 Current state value stream map with improvement opportunities (a.k.a. future state).

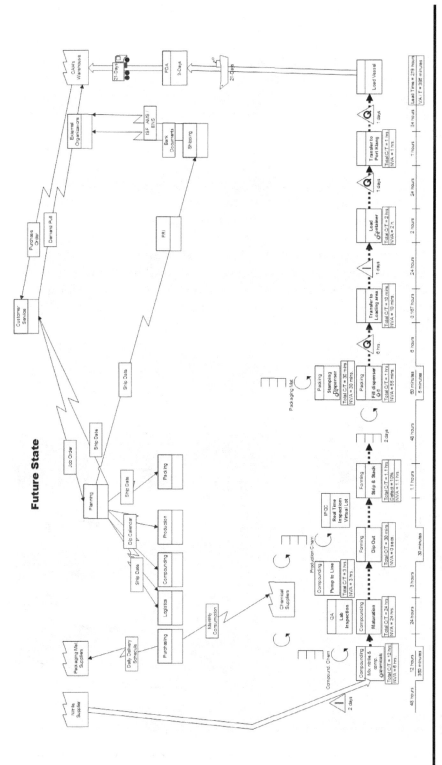

Figure 1.25 Ideal state value stream map.

Within 8 hours, we had fully mapped the offshore upstream oil delivery process and populated multiple pages of "parking lot" notes, all of which would be addressed over the following few days. Utilizing a digital camera (this was before the proliferation of smart phones), we captured the manually created, post-it laden process as our "draft" baseline. It would remain a "draft" until all parking-lot items were resolved. (A recreation of the manually created current state VSM is shown in Figure 1.26. Recreated in Visio.)

We had thus established a VSM PLT. The following day, the same group started brainstorming improvement opportunities. We started with a current state VSM with a PLT above 20 days. We spent several hours of unconstrained brainstorming of improvement opportunities with a goal of reducing the PLT to as low as possible. We collected all brainstormed improvement ideas on post-it notes. We created over 50 potential improvement ideas and then utilized Affinity Diagramming as a method to organize the ideas into groups. After affinization of the ideas, we created four groups of related ideas (>50 ideas to four groups) and utilized a waterfall chart to show the proposed future state target (Figure 1.27).

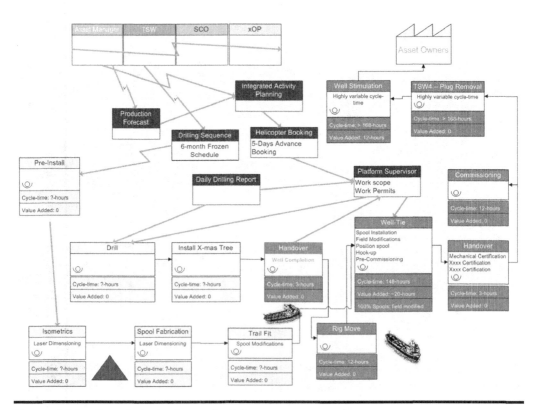

Figure 1.26   Case-in-Point Example 1.9 current state value stream map.

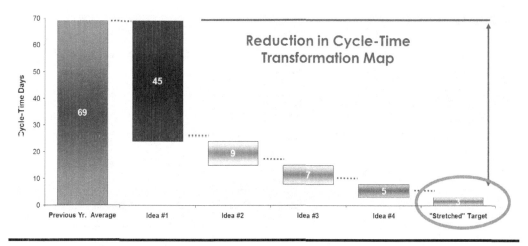

Figure 1.27   Waterfall chart – targeted future state.

SIPOC

SIPOC is an acronym for Suppliers–Inputs–Process–Outputs–Customers. SIPOC is a tool that summarizes the inputs and outputs of one or more processes in a tabular form.

A SIPOC can be deployed early in the assessment to help identify potential team members and/or stakeholders. The outputs are the metrics which will be used to measure the project; the inputs allow the project team to consider various potential critical process-drivers. And, of course, the process itself provides the stop–start barriers (i.e. the transformation's scope). A SIPOC helps define a complex project that may not be well scoped.

A SIPOC (like most Lean tools) is best competed by a cross-functional team. The team should brainstorm all the variables that are relevant to a given process (Figure 1.28).

There are many ways that you can structure your SIPOC diagram; Figure 1.29 shows my favorite template because it requests the relevant metrics.

Another acceptable SIPOC format can be seen in Figure 1.30.

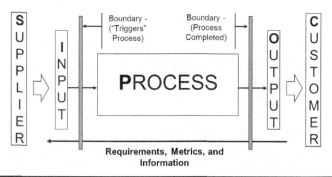

Figure 1.28   SIPOC.

SIPOC TEMPLATE

Process:

Suppliers	Inputs	Major Process Steps	Outputs	Customers

Input Metrics	Process Metrics	Output Metrics	
			Safety
			Quality
			Delivery
			Cost
			Other
			Other

Figure 1.29   SIPOC template #1.

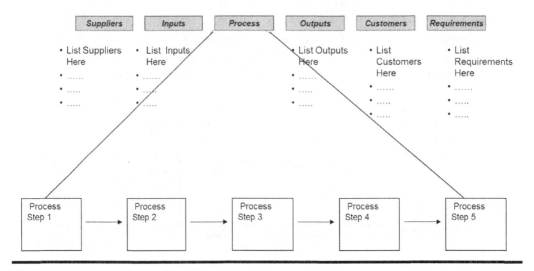

SIPOC Diagram

Figure 1.30   SIPOC template #2.

Case-in-Point Example 1.10 SIPOC Examples

Figure 1.31 shows a simple SIPOC for the subassembly operation of a metal fabricated part assembly for a US OEM of industrial equipment. This SIPOC was used to establish the scope and identify the stakeholders for a project to improve the process lead time and to establish the kanban and supermarket sizing to decouple the subassembly process for the final unit assembly and ensure no subassembly shortages at final assembly.

Figure 1.32 shows a SIPOC for a medical glove order fulfillment process from a Malaysian glove manufacturer to an US customer. This SIPOC was used to establish the scope and identify the stakeholders for a project to improve the order fulfillment process lead time (PLT). Additionally, it identified the key metrics so that a data collection plan (a.k.a. measurement plan) could be created and the data collection process initiated. This completed project resulted in a 15% reduction of the order fulfillment PLT, from 59.2 days to 50.3 days. After a full assessment of all the operating cost factors; the gross margins were improved by 30% (from 10% to 13%).

SWOT

In a transformation initiative, it's always good to evaluate your organization's strengths and the effect that external factors have on these (especially effective for assisting in assessing the competitive landscape).

The structure of a generic SWOT is shown in Figure 1.33.

- Strengths describe the positive attributes of your organization. They are within your control. A strength should address a critical customer need. Customers should be defined as internal or external.
- Weaknesses are aspects of your business that detract from the value you offer or place you at a competitive disadvantage.

SIPOC Diagram

Subassembly "X": weld & assembly

Suppliers	Inputs	Process	Outputs	Customers
		Laser Cut Sheets		
Material Control	Work Order Tag	Press Brake		
Metal Fab Shop / Kanban	Fabricated Parts	Stud – Tack Weld	Subassembly "X"	Product "X" Final Assembly Workstation
		Robot Assembly Weld		
External Suppliers / Kanban	Purchased Parts	Hardware Attach		
External Suppliers / Kanban	Sheet Metal	Leak Test		
		Polish / Paint		

Figure 1.31   Example - SIPOC diagram: Metal fabricated part assembly.

SIPOC

Process:	**Medical Glove Manufacturing - Malaysia**			

Suppliers	Inputs	Major Process Steps	Outputs	Customers
Supplier "A" - Thailand	Nitrile (Latex)	Compounding	Nitrile Compound	
Supplier "B" - Malaysia	Glove Molds	Forming	Finished Glove	
	Finished Glove	Storage - Supermarket		
Supplier "G" - Malaysia	Glove Dispenser Box	Packaging	Gloves in Dispenser in Cardboard Carton	
Supplier "C" - Malaysia	Cardboard Cartons			
Supplier "D" - Malaysia	Shipping Container	Container Loading	Shipping Bill-of-Lading	
Supplier "D" - Malaysia	3rd Party Trucker	Trucking to Port		
	Shipping Bill-of-Lading			
Supplier "E" - Malaysia	3rd Party Container Ship	Sea-ship to USA	Shipping Bill-of-Lading	
	Container	FDA Inspection		
Supplier "F" - USA	3rd Party Trucker	Ground transport to Customer Warehouse	Invoice	Customer "A"
	Malaysian Manufacturer		Medical Gloves	

Input Metrics	Process Metrics	Output Metrics	
	First Aid / Lost-Time		Safety
	Defects per Million Gloves	FDA Acceptance Rate	Quality

	Process Lead-time		Delivery
Nitrile Cost/Kg (wet)	Cost-to-Manufacture	Average Selling Price	Cost
Packaging Cost	Manufacturing Variance	Gross Margins	Cost

	Shipping Cost		Other

Figure 1.32   Example - SIPOC diagram: Order fulfillment process.

■ Opportunities are positive external factors. Opportunities relate to positive or favorable current or future advantage or trend. Opportunities represent reasons your business is likely to prosper.

■ Threats relate to an unfavorable situation, trend, or change. Threats are external factors beyond your control that could place your strategy, or the business itself, at risk. You have no control over these, but you may benefit by having contingency plans to address them.

So, a SWOT should help you determine …

■ how to sustain and/or maximize your strengths;
■ what the drivers of your weaknesses are and how to overcome them;
■ how to effectively maximize your opportunities;
■ how to minimize or avoid potential threats.

Strengths	Weaknesses
• Current competitiveness differentiators (advantages) • Operational advantages • What metrics are you best at; i.e. Safety, Quality, Delivery and/or Cost? • From Customers' perspective; what are your strengths?	• What do you need to improve? • What metrics are your worst at; i.e. Safety, Quality, Delivery and/or Cost? • What loses your sales and/or market share? • From your Customers' perspective; what are your weaknesses?
Opportunities	Threats
• How do you leverage your strengths to seize new opportunities? • What weaknesses can you eliminate to open-up more opportunities? • What are your Political, Economical, Socio-Cultural and Technological opportunities?	• What obstacles are you currently facing? • Any threatening trends in Government or Regulatory? • Are any of your Weaknesses threatening your successes? • What are your Political, Economical, Socio-Cultural and Technological threats?

Figure 1.33   Generic SWOT diagram structure.

Case-in-Point Example 1.11 SWOT Example

We had a client that was a highly diversified US Fortune 100 company that asked us to assess one of their major divisions, their Semiconductor Product Group. So, an initial step was to assess what their perceived (and actual) internal strengths and weaknesses were, and what positive and/or negative external factors they must be prepared to take advantage of or to have contingencies to offset. (Note: this SWOT was created circa 1999, so the opportunities and threats have probably changed.) (Figure 1.34).

PROCESS MAPPING

A process map is a tool to visually illustrate the flow of the product/service. The purpose of process mapping is for better understanding. It involves the gathering and organization of facts about the work (data can be extracted from related RBWA) and displaying them so that they can be questioned and improved by the stakeholders.

The RBWA is a technique to employ while documenting the detailed process by completing a walk-through of the process while pretending to be the product or service. The RBWA should engage the associates who are performing the process.

Once the project team has "walked" the process, creating the process map – or picturing the process – provides the visual documentation.

Figure 1.35 shows the common symbols used in process mapping.

Strengths	Weaknesses
• Management support & overall leadership • TPM program • Quality & yield – incoming wafer • Quality & yield of backend assembly & test process • Short order fulfillment lead-times (large buffer inventories) • Integrated device manufacturer (own wafer, assembly, test & OEM)	• Layout constraints (centralized molding) • Long Manufacturing Process Lead-Time • Poor data management / ERP system • Large lot sizes • Wafer fab in US; long transit times and inventories
Opportunities	**Threats**
• Customer demand management – too much volatility • Customer demanding shorter lead-times • Mobile phone market is exponentially growing	• Competition – devices are mainly commodity (easy market entry) • Most devices are not leading-edge technology (no competitive advantage) • Wafer foundry landscape shifting from US to Taiwan and Korea • Fabless & pure-foundry options

A SWOT diagram, circa 1999, for an US Fortune 100 OEM manufacturer.

Figure 1.34 A competitive landscape SWOT example.

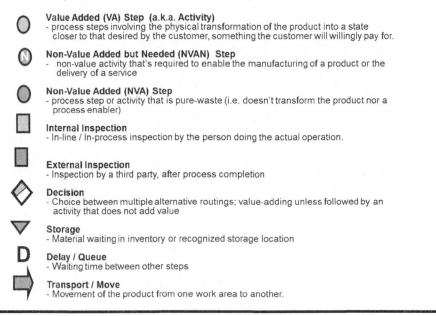

Value Added (VA) Step (a.k.a. Activity)
- process steps involving the physical transformation of the product into a state closer to that desired by the customer, something the customer will willingly pay for.

Non-Value Added but Needed (NVAN) Step
- non-value activity that's required to enable the manufacturing of a product or the delivery of a service

Non-Value Added (NVA) Step
- process step or activity that is pure-waste (i.e. doesn't transform the product nor a process enabler)

Internal Inspection
- In-line / In-process inspection by the person doing the actual operation.

External Inspection
- Inspection by a third party, after process completion

Decision
- Choice between multiple alternative routings; value-adding unless followed by an activity that does not add value

Storage
- Material waiting in inventory or recognized storage location

Delay / Queue
- Waiting time between other steps

Transport / Move
- Movement of the product from one work area to another.

Figure 1.35 Common process mapping symbols.

Case-in-Point Example 1.12 Process Mapping

The process map shown in Figure 1.36 is for a wafer-fab sub-activity. The top-level activity is one element of a Value Stream Map, but the process map breaks that element down into sub-elements (or sub-activities) for further analysis. The total element had a process lead time of 11.1 days, and further analysis reveals that only 2.7 days are value added, while delays (29%) and

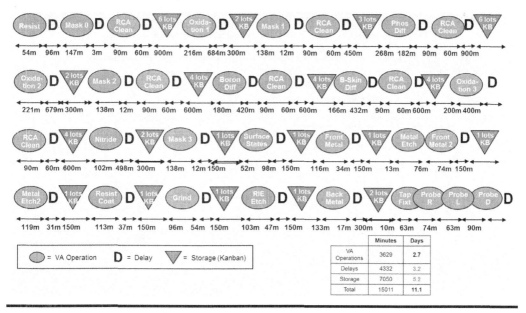

Figure 1.36   Wafer-fab sub-activity process map.

storage (47%) were the largest part of the overall process lead time, which shows a huge opportunity for improvement.

The details for the Process Map was extracted from a RBWA (Figure 1.36).

TRIPLE PLAY CHART

An analysis tool that may not be as common as some of the others is the "Triple Play Chart". The name is derived from the comparison of three variables on one chart: production, shipments, and finished goods inventory. The objective is to assess the synchronization of those three variables (Figure 1.37).

Case-in-Point Example 1.13 Triple Play Chart

This case story highlights how a Triple Play Chart can be utilized in a Lean Transformation Assessment. We had a consulting client with an obvious issue of too much inventory and inventory turns in the single digits (<10).

Our overall assessment revealed that there were many causes: e.g. large batch sizes, building to forecast, just-in-case inventories, long process lead times, etc.

One of the assessment tools that we always utilized was the Triple Play Chart. We chose the highest volume SKU (device) that they were producing at that time; I needed a plot of weekly production quantities, weekly customer shipments, and a finished goods inventory.

Figure 1.38 shows the Triple Play Chart of that plot.

Triple Play Chart

Goal: Analyze the current level of synchronization between inventory, demand & production.

Choose two (2) stock keeping units(SKU) from the products in scope and provide the following data.
One SKU should be high-volume (Annual volume within top 10% of commodity group).
The other SKU should be low-volume (Annual volume within bottom 10% of commodity group).
Need data for a 52-week period (beginning at any week).

SKU: _____

Report all data in quantity of devices

Weeks	Inventory Level (Finished Goods)	Demand (Shipments)	Production Run Rate
1			
2			
3			
4			
5			
6			
7			
8			
9			
10			
11			
12			

Figure 1.37 Triple play assessment tool.

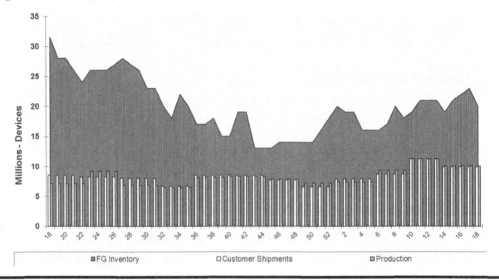

Figure 1.38 Case-in-Point Example 1.13 triple play graph #1.

The customer shipments and the production output were very close to synchronized. But the purple mountain of finished goods inventory remained high throughout the 52-week snapshot. They were doing a good job of managing the production to customer requirements, but finished goods was going unmanaged.

This chart was shared with the Senior VP of Operations, and he went ballistic. His team really had no explanation for the huge amount of finished

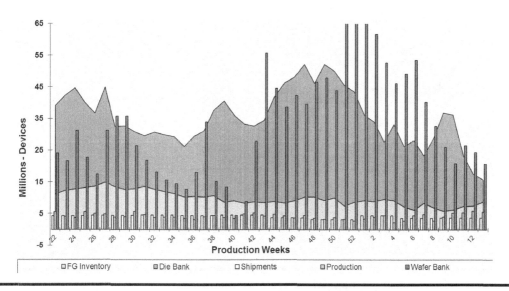

Figure 1.39   Case-in-Point Example 1.13 triple play graph #2.

goods inventory. But no problem, as the cellular manufacturing and one-piece flow (i.e. one-lot flow) solution that was ultimately implemented addressed and eliminated overproduction. But this "purple mountain" remained infamous at this company.

Another Triple Play Chart that we created was actually a "Five Play", as there were large in-process storage areas for incoming semiconductor wafers (a.k.a. wafer-bank); after the wafers were diced and probed, they were stored in a die-bank. The graph in Figure 1.39 reflects the results of our assessment:

■ Once again, production and shipments were fairly synchronized (and are reflected in Figure 1.39 as those tiny yellow and white columns).
■ Finished goods inventory (light surface area) was consistently high throughout the 52-week snapshot.
■ The wafer-bank (dark columns) inventory was volatile and reflects a lot of unevenness.
■ The red surface area reflected the die-bank, which far exceeds the production and/or shipments.
■ Bottom line is that there's no correlation of inventory at any stage or customer shipments.

So, the Triple Play Charts highlight gaps between inventory and customer requirements and identify opportunities for improvement.

FINANCIAL ANALYSIS

In the initial analysis of a company's transformational initiative, it's important to get a snapshot of the company's financials. At the start of the assessment, you'll take a quick look at a company's Profit and Loss and Balance Sheet. For

Financial Analysis

Materials		Direct Labor		Staff & Indirect Labor		Overhead	
Please indicate sub-totals by major material families		Include only wages and benefits. Please indicate sub-totals by department.		Include only wages and benefits. Please indicate sub-totals by department or function, including:		All other cost, including:	
Description	Value	Description	Value	Description	Value	Description	Value
				Sales & Marketing		Occupancy*	
				Engineering		Process Utilities (Energy, Water, Waste Processing)	
				Planning & Production Control		Equipment Depreciation	
				Supervision		Financing	
				Material Handling (Including Warehouse & Receiving)			
				Shipping			
				Maintenance			
				After Sales Service			
				Quality Assurance & Control			
				Document Reproduction			

Figure 1.40 Example – Financial analysis template.

us, this is a company's operational transformation assessment, so we wouldn't be doing an in-depth financial analysis at this time. Initially, we're looking for "the vital few and the trivial many" (see A-B-C Analysis below). We're trying to identify the biggest opportunities for improvement (Figure 1.40).

COST OF QUALITY

Cost of quality is a methodology to determine the extent to which resources are used for activities that prevent poor quality, appraise the quality of the organization's products or services, and result from internal and external failures. I guess cost of quality has become old terminology, as it most often referred to today as cost of poor quality (COPQ).

Cost of quality has two main components: the cost of good quality (or the cost of conformance) and the cost of poor quality (or the cost of non-conformance).

Cost of quality can be broken down to:
- **Cost of Good Quality (Prevention and Appraisal Costs)**
  - Prevention Costs (cost to do it right the first time)
    - training;
    - quality department costs;
    - process monitoring;
    - quality improvement initiatives;
    - supplier evaluations and development.
  - Appraisal Costs
    - inspection and testing of incoming material;
    - inspection and testing (in-process, final, etc.);
    - product, process, and/or service audits;
    - calibration of measuring and test equipment.

- **Cost of Poor Quality (Internal and External Failure Costs)**
  - Internal Failure Costs
    - rework;
    - repairs;
    - scrap.
  - External Failure Costs
    - complaint management;
    - returns and/or replacements;
    - warranties;
    - loss of sales or customer goodwill.

Case-in-Point Example 1.14 Cost of Quality

During the assessment phase of a transformation initiative, you probably won't do an in-depth cost of quality analysis; however, you will want to identify the major buckets of the cost of quality and, in particular, identify the cost of poor quality (e.g. rework, repair, scrap, warranties, customer returns, etc.). The cost of poor quality would not be readily prevalent on a P&L or Balance Sheet. Obtaining yield, scrap, and rework data is usually fairly is easy as most companies monitor this in some form. The key is to convert (quantitate) these metrics into a monetary value ($). In the assessment phase, you want to differentiate the vital few from the trivial many. A Lean Transformation is a long, continuous journey, so you want to prioritize your transformation focus on the high impact areas (i.e. items that provide the greatest benefit to customer and company). You'll also need to weigh the effort for the benefit. You'll want a transformation scope that can be completed (realized) within 12 to 16 months, so you must include an evaluation of the required effort before including something in the scope of your Lean Transformation initiative. The metaphor that you'll often hear in regards to scope is "don't try to boil the ocean".

Here's a recent scenario that I want to share with you. I encountered a couple of engineers working very diligently on separate complex yield improvement initiatives. Both engineers are highly intelligent and very passionate about their projects, BUT, as I got a chance to look at their projects, it became evident very quickly that these were complex (high effort) projects addressing problems that would yield minimum financial impact upon resolution, and that any solutions/discoveries that came from these projects would be unlikely to be replicable to other products or processes. These were relatively low-return projects. In these two instances, the application of the Pareto principle to overall yield and scrap data before starting/choosing these projects would clearly have shown other opportunities that were better impact initiatives (i.e. bang for the buck). I think all companies have limited engineering resources, so it's imperative to correctly prioritize your initiatives – and this prioritization must include all key stakeholders.

A-B-C ANALYSIS

A-B-C Analysis is a data stratification methodology to distinguish the important (a.k.a. critical) from the unimportant (a.k.a. trivial). The origin can be traced back to Pareto's Law or the Pareto principle. The Pareto principle is a principle, named after economist Vilfredo Pareto, that specifies an unequal relationship between inputs and outputs. This is often called the 80/20 Rule, as 80% of an input or output is aligned with a 20% output or input respectively. Examples could be:

■ 80% of your problems are the output of 20% of your actions (inputs);
■ 80% of a company's revenue is derived from 20% of the company's product;
■ 80% of a company's defects are created on 20% of the company's product;
■ 20% of a company's SKU*s account for 80% of the company's inventory (value, days-on-hand, demand, etc.);
■ 20% of a company's purchased items (#) equates to 80% of the company's total spend ($).

And so on ...

The breakout is seldom exactly 80/20 or 20/80, but it is some type of proportional range: 70/30, 75/25, etc.

The significance of the Pareto principle was notably supported by Dr. Joseph Juran, who is credited with the statement "the vital few and the trivial many". This means that you should be focused on a few vital items that are the majority of your problem or will provide the majority of the benefit, rather than focusing on a large number of items that will provide trivial benefit.

A couple of the best applications of A-B-C stratification are inventory management and procurement strategies:

■ In inventory management, basically using the Pareto principle, you can expect that approximately 20% of your SKUs will equal 80% on the demand consumption. So, determine your 20% point: this represents the "vital few", or where your focus should be: i.e. the As. Cs would be the majority of SKUs, approximately 70%, but only about 5~10% of the annual demand; Bs would be approximately 10% of your

---

* SKU is an acronym for "stock-keeping unit", which is defined as a distinct item being purchased, produced, delivered, or sold. A more simplified definition would simply be a part number for any distinct item.

SKUs and 5~10% of the annual demand. A-B-C allows you to establish different replenishment strategies, safety stock calculations, days-on-hand (DOH) stocking targets, cycle-count schemes, etc. for each of the A-B-C stratifications.

■ For procurement strategies, your As would be approximately 20% of your SKUs, which should equate to about 80% of your annual spend; again, your vital few. In procurement, you would want to differentiate your procurement (acquisition) method, inventory targets, replenishment scheme, etc. strategies based on the A-B-C stratification. A key reason for doing this is that typically (traditionally) your acquisition costs will be the same for each SKU or commodity; a typical scenario could be that a purchase order is costing you $500 to administer, and you'd be spending this for your vital few as well as your trivial many. But common sense tells you that you must reduce your acquisition costs for the trivial many; you must consider vendor-managed stock/replenishment schemes, blanket purchase orders, procurement (p) cards, pay-on-consumption, etc.

Case-in-Point Example 1.15 Product Portfolio Analysis (A-B-C Analysis)

One application of A-B-C Analysis in the assessment phase of a transformation initiative is a Product Portfolio Analysis. The case story that I'm going to use here is for a Japanese global-brand consumer goods manufacturer; this story is centered around one of this company's Southeast Asia R&D and manufacturing centers (a Center of Excellence for a specific range of residential and commercial air conditioners). Our initialassessment revealed that this site had an amazing 1300-plus finished product SKUs for its residential air conditioning portfolio. That seems to be a plethora of air conditioning products. Maintaining a high variable portfolio of any product comes with high overhead costs, so an initial analysis of a diversified, extensive portfolio such as this is a A-B-C stratification based on annual demand (sales volume) for each SKU.

We first create a file (Excel) of all SKUs versus the sales volume generated by each SKU; then we sorted the SKUs (in Excel) by sales volume (highest to lowest). Then we added an Excel column that will be the percent of total sales volume that each SKU represents. So, now we have a nice baseline: each SKU, its annual sales volume, and the percent of total sales volume attributed to each SKU. To start the analysis, we'll create a new Excel column that will represent the accumulative sales volume for the full portfolio of individual SKUs; then, the final spreadsheet development task is to create an accumulative summary of the total sales volume.

Figure 1.41 shows an excerpt of an example Excel A-B-C stratification sheet.

This analysis revealed that we had 1,300 finished goods SKU, but 547 (42%) of these SKUs not only had zero sales volume the past 12 months but also had none forecasted for the next 12 months – yet they remained active SKUs. As I didn't want these dormant SKUs to skew my analysis, I ignored them in my A-B-C analysis. So, my base number of SKUs became 753, and my A-B-C stratification revealed that the A classification consisted of 90 SKUs (12%), which was 80% of the sales volumes; the B classification consisted of 105 SKUs (14%) and 10% of the sales volume; and the C classification consisted of 548 SKUs (74%) and 10% of the sales volume (Figure 1.42).

No	SKU	Item Description	Sales-Volume	% Sales-Volume	Cummmulative Sales-Volume	Cummmulative %
1	xxxx-01-10421	Item xxxxxx	2402061	2.83%	2402061	2.8%
2	xxxx-01-01141	Item xxxxxx	2033070	2.40%	4435131	5.2%
3	xxxx-01-00011	Item xxxxxx	1886864	2.23%	6321995	7.5%
4	xxxx-01-10001	Item xxxxxx	1818094	2.14%	8140089	9.6%
5	xxxx-10-00020	Item xxxxxx	1596000	1.88%	9736089	11.5%
6	xxxx-15-10008	Item xxxxxx	1153778	1.36%	10889867	12.8%

Figure 1.41 Excerpt of an Excel A-B-C stratification sheet.

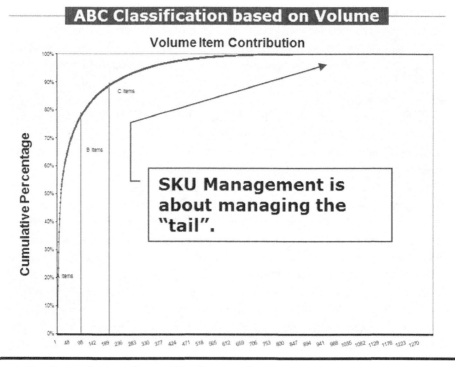

Figure 1.42 Example A-B-C stratification graph.

Chapter 2

Lean – The Relentless Pursuit to Eliminate Waste

Muda, Muri, & Mura

I guess that there are many definitions and perspectives as to what Lean really means in the business environment, but the simplest definition of Lean is "the relentless pursuit to eliminate waste". "Waste" can be categorized as any non-valued-added activity; and a non-value-added activity is any activity that doesn't add direct value to the customer – but more on that a little later.

An expanded definition of Lean would be:

> *Lean represents the use (or consumption) of no more of any resource than the minimum required to produce a product or provide a service to the expectations of the customer.*

Or to restate slightly differently:

> *Lean means that you only use the minimal amount of human labor, the minimal amount of utilities, the minimal amount of direct/indirect materials, the minimal amount of space, etc. that is required to produce a product or provide a service to the expectations of the customer.*

So, as you think about these statements, it may make you think that Lean is just common sense. And I would totally agree with you. Who wouldn't want a company to produce a product or provide a service with the minimal amount of resources possible?

And this is where Lean Transformation enters. Lean Transformation takes common sense practices and then makes them a common practice; it makes them your culture ... a continuous improvement culture. In future chapters of this book, we will look at the common sense practices that are the building blocks of Lean, how we effectively integrate these Lean building blocks into a common practice within your business, and how to use these building blocks to transform your business.

I started my first Lean Transformation back in 1979. I definitely had never heard of Lean, as that terminology was not coined until the 1990s, and I only had a basic knowledge of some "just-in-time" methodologies that were being deployed by companies in Japan. And I didn't hear of the Toyota Production System until much, much later in life when I took on a role as a consultant. So, my first Lean Transformation started as simply trying to produce telecommunication equipment at the highest quality level as fast as possible to meet customer demand, and to do so at the lowest possible cost (which easily translates into producing telecommunication equipment utilizing the minimal number of resources possible). And as engineer, that was all common sense to me. So, as my early years as an engineer and as a manager of manufacturing engineering, my Lean journey was based on trial and error; my team and I made many mistakes, but we always learned from these trials. And we relied heavily on common sense. It was simple: our goal was to simplify the processes and reduce cost by minimizing the number of resources utilized.

Now, with the inception of Lean, we started to institutionalize "common sense" and establish a structured methodology for assessing activities and identifying improvement opportunities.

As I have repeatedly stated, Lean is about the relentless elimination of all types of wastes. Now that we have defined Lean, let's take a deeper dive into defining waste.

It's widely accepted (and highlighted by the Toyota Production System) that there are three forms of waste: muda, muri, and mura. And as you probably know, or realized, muda, muri, and mura are Japanese terms.

- *Muda*, in English, is simply translated as pure waste and is most often referred to as the "seven deadly wastes". These seven deadly wastes are transportation, inventory, motion, waiting, overproduction, over-processing, and defects (TIMWOOD). I'll address all of these in detail later in this chapter. Within this book, waste and muda shall be interchangeable, although I will most prominently use *waste* as my terminology of choice. So, waste (muda) can also be defined as any non-value-adding activity, and as any activity that consumes resources without creating value for the customer.

■ *Muri*, in English, is simply translated as overburden. However, muri's translation should be expanded beyond overburden to include unreasonableness: i.e. beyond "reasonable" limits. And "reasonable" means being within the bounds of common sense, being non-excessive or non-extreme. So, from the perspective of Lean, the objective is to eliminate overburdening of equipment and people, or to eliminate unreasonable demands and/or expectations of equipment and people.

Muri is the overburdening of resources, e.g. equipment, people, and systems. Overburdening can also be defined as requiring resources to perform at a more demanding pace than the equipment or systems design, or at a pace/volume greater than that for which the workforce was sized and/or managed.

Examples of muri include:
– demand that exceeds process or equipment capacities;
– having associates working on processes that they are not trained on;
– poorly laid out workstations, etc. (causes muda);
– demand variations (mura);
– unclear written or verbal instructions;
– lack of proper tools and equipment;
– lack of proper maintenance/unreliable equipment;
– unreliable processes;
– poor ergonomics anywhere.

Case-in-Point Example 2.1 Overburdening Operators' Physical Capabilities (Muri)

Here's an example of muri that I'd like to share with you. The activity was called "cuffing a glove". One day on a Gemba Walk, it was noted that the fixtures used by the various operators to "cuff a glove" varied significantly between workstations; we noticed that there were variations in the activities being performed by the operators. Our initial step was to standardize the operation; in our initial meeting with a small group of selected "cuffing" operators, we discovered than many of the operators were having physical medical problems that were being caused by the "stress" that the design of some of these workstations were putting on their wrists. The workstation layouts were causing carpal tunnel syndrome (i.e. overburdening the operators' physical capabilities). We found evidence of muri in our workstation designs and our fixtures; the lack of proper job instructions (or Standard Work) compounded the issue. Our initial series of workshops with different groups of operators led to a standardized workstation and fixture design, which were later evaluated against ergonomic best principles/practices. So, after a new workstation/fixture design was prototyped, evaluated, and confirmed, the team of operators, engineers, etc. started developing a corresponding set of Standard Work (especially the Job Element Breakdown Sheet, which would be the individual station job instructions). After a short pilot run to prove the new design, the new workstation design, fixture, and Standard Work were replicated throughout the department. These changes removed the overburdening of the operators' physical capabilities.

■ Mura, in English, mean unevenness. It can be further defined as variability, inconsistency, erraticness, irregularity, or lack of uniformity within any business processes. Process variabilities and irregularities will invariably be key drivers of all types of muda and muri, and mura can often be caused by muda and muri; I guess it's the old "chicken–egg" scenario when it comes to deciding if mura caused muri or muda or if muri or muda caused mura. No worries: solving one will reduce or eliminate the others. Just identify the waste (muda, muri, or muda), and eliminate or minimize them all.

A common manifestation of mura is fluctuations in customer demand, which invariably leads to unevenness in production. But this unevenness is often caused by internal production systems or policies and not true customer demand. In addition, mura can be the result of varying periods of hyperactivity or lulls (bottlenecks or equipment or process idleness).

Case-in-Point Example 2.2 Leveling Customer Demand (Mura)

During the initial mobile phone craze in the late nineties, we had a client that produced a power transistor (SOT) for one of the largest mobile phone manufacturers at that time. This customer would place monthly orders for a million+ devices; our client would then load this order into their system, which would create a single delivery date for the entire order within their quoted delivery times (X days). This would create tremendous burden on production operations (mura). But as we discussed the situation with our client, common sense suggested that this OEM phone manufacturer didn't really need or probably want all one million devices at one time – the phone manufacturer was probably also trying to level load its manufacturing over the month. And since these devices were physically very small, all customer shipments were by air. We worked with our client to create a simple proposal: they would produce the month's demand evenly over the month and shipments would initially be made weekly. When the customer was offered this proposal, they accepted immediately, as this fit their just-in-time philosophy even better. Shortly after implementing this new weekly-shipment scheme, common sense prevailed again, and shipments started being made daily, as the air freight cost was the same and the manufacturer (client) and customer could both reduce inventory levels accordingly. This eliminated unevenness for both the manufacturer and their customer, thus creating a win–win for both parties. The solution was simply better communication and collaboration between supplier and customer.

Value Added vs. Non-Value Added

One of the definitions that we used above for muda (waste) was any non-value-added activity.

So, let's first differentiate value added from non-value added.

It's also important to think about activities as being either value added vs. non-value added.

A value-added activity is …

■ the part of manufacturing that your customer is willing to pay for (i.e. an activity that changes form, fit, or function);
■ an activity that if skipped would affect the value/performance of the product;
■ an activity that must be done right the first time.

A non-value-added activity is an activity that simply doesn't create value for the customer. Non-value-added activities can be distinguished as either "needed" or "not needed".

A non-value-added activity may be classified as "needed" if …

■ it cannot be eliminated based on the current state of technology or thinking;
■ it is required by regulatory, legal, or customer mandates; or
■ it's necessary due to the non-robustness of the process currently required; current risk tolerance.

Additionally, a plethora of administrative activities fall into the non-value-added but needed category: invoicing customers for payment, purchasing materials, etc., creating shipping documents, regulatory reporting, etc.

Any "not needed" non-value added is most often simply defined as a waste. All of the traditional waste categories (a.k.a. TIMWOOD) fall into this category; as we know, waste is any unnecessary activity or the excessive use of a resource. So, any activity in this category should be targeted for elimination.

However, it can be argued that this segregation isn't really necessary, because if an activity is non-value added, then it's not important if it's needed or not, as the goal in either case is to minimize or eliminate. But since a large percentage (as much as 80~99%) of any business or manufacturing process is non-value-added activities, it's beneficial to further segregate non-value-added activities into "needed" or "not needed"; this will help prioritize the "not needed", as the removal of "not needed" may achieve positive benefit with less effort than required to eliminate/minimize a "needed" non-value-added activity.

Figure 2.1 provides a more detailed differentiation of these categories of activities.

Now, on to learning more about the characteristics of waste.

Value-Added	Non-Value Added: Needed	Non-Value Added

• Changes the form, fit or function of a product
• The parts of a process that the Customer would be willing to pay-for.
• Any activity that is perceived as value-adding by the Customer.
• Any activity if skipped would affect the value / performance of the product or service.
• Examples:
  – Assembly
  – Parametric Testing
  – Internal Inspection or testing*
  – Packing & Shipping
  – Machining
  – Painting
 	
Inspection or testing of own work. Quality-at-the-Source.
	• Activities creating no-value but required the product out the door AND which cannot be eliminated based on the current state of thinking or technology
	• Required by regulatory, legal or mandated by Customer
	• Necessary due to non-robustness of a process
	• Examples:
	  – Training
	  – Checking Chemical Properties; e.g. Viscosity, pH, Temperature, etc.
	  – Measurement Conformance
	  – Point-of-Use Material
	  – Order Entry / Processing
	  – Invoicing / Billing
	  – Purchasing
	  – Regulatory Reporting
		• **Waste** – any unnecessary activity or excessive use of a resource
		• Activities that should be eliminated as they're creating no value for the Customer
		• Any activity that is perceived as value-adding by the Customer.
		• Any just-in-case action or resource; e.g. inspections, inventories, etc.
		• Examples:
		  – TIMWOOD (8-wastes)
		  – External Inspection
		  – Testing for defects or spec nonconformance
		  – "Re's" ... Rework, Returns, Redo, Reinspect, Repair, Rewrite, Reassess, Reinsert, Reevaluate, etc.

Figure 2.1 Characterization of value-added vs. non-value added: Needed vs. non-value added.

Waste – Any Amount that's More Than the Minimum Required

Waste is the usage/consumption of any resources more than the minimum required to produce a product or deliver a service to the expectations of the customer. Typically, we'll see symptoms of waste before we actually identify the waste and its causes (as illustrated in Figure 2.2).

In talking about Lean waste, we almost always turn to the so-called seven deadly wastes (TIMWOOD):

- transportation;
- inventory;
- motion;
- wait;
- overproduction;
- over-processing;
- wait.

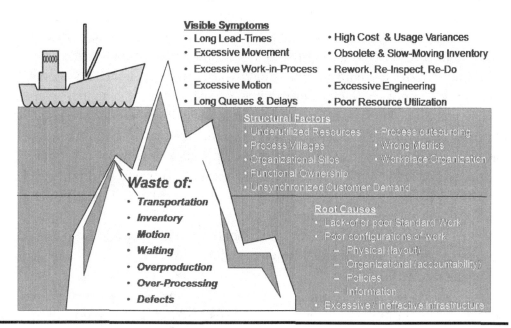

Figure 2.2 Waste – Visible symptoms vs. hidden factors & causes.

These have been described in a few different ways, but their origin is most often credited to Taiichi Ohno and his book *Toyota Production System – Beyond Large-Scale Production*.

Ohno stated that the preliminary step for the application of the Toyota Product System is the identification of waste, which he categorized as:

- waste of overproduction;
- waste of time on hand (waiting);
- waste in transportation;
- waste of processing itself (he further categorized this as "too much machining (overproduction)");
- waste of stock on hand (inventory);
- waste of movement;
- waste of making defective products.

These seven categories of waste became one of the key mantras of the Lean nation: the seven deadly wastes. However, I think there was an oversight by a large portion of the self-proclaimed Lean nation. Ohno didn't state anything that truly limits the types of potential process wastes to those seven categories; instead, these were seven logical waste categories to help guide Lean Practitioners in their quest to identify and eliminate waste. Over the years, Lean "experts" have tried to add many additional waste categories: administrative (paperwork reports, etc.); waste of resources (people and space); underutilized resources; wrong metrics; resistance to change; wasted talent; transactional errors; environmental/utility waste; inappropriate IT systems; overuse of technology; lack of creativity; confusion; unsafe activities, etc.

The category that has consistently seemed to stick is ineffective use of resources, with "resources" expanded to include space, equipment, people, or any resource used to produce a product or provide a service. Ineffective utilization of resource has been added to waste acronyms such as "DOWNTIME" as "N" (non-utilization of resources) and TIM R WOOD/ TRIMWOOD, etc. as "R" (resource waste).

You'll see many blogs, articles, etc. debate the value of adding more categories of waste. I will contest, however, that a proliferation of waste categories is itself a waste.

We should be focused simply on eliminating wastes, and waste should be defined as the utilization of any resources beyond the very minimum required to a produce a given part or provide a given service. It's that simple. Resources should be fully encompassing: space, direct/indirect labor, materials, information, utilities …

The obvious argument would be that I missed the eighth, "newest" waste category, but I will contend that non-utilization of resources is not a waste but rather a blasphemous infraction of one of the basic principles of the Toyota Production System: respect for people. If my overall objective is to ensure that the minimum number of resources are utilized, then this encompasses the supposedly ineffective use of resources.

So, going forward, I say let's use these categories as guidelines to help us identify waste but not allow them to become a barrier to expanding our relentless pursuit of waste elimination. Let's use these categories to practice our skills in seeing and recognizing waste; we must learn to recognize waste in all of its forms.

So, in my discussion of waste in this book, I'm going to revert back 15 years or so and go with seven categories of waste (the original seven deadly wastes) and the waste of acronym of TIMWOOD. However, I equally don't think we should put too much emphasis on the categories, instead maintaining greater focus on the relentless pursuit to ensure that we utilize the very minimum number of resources required to achieve maximum value for the customers.

The only additional waste that I think is worth thinking about is the idea that "not striving to improve a process but rather to maintain the status quo is a waste". So, let's proceed to understand how the seven deadly wastes hinder the performance of our processes and businesses.

TIMWOOD (Figure 2.3)

<u>T</u>IMWOOD: *Transportation*

Transportation waste is any movement of material that adds no value to the product and/or customer. Transportation waste can be the result of transportation in the form of carts, trucks, fork-trucks, human, or conveyors; airplanes or boats may be modes of non-value-adding transportation.

Transportation waste is often the result of poor (non-optimized) factory or office layouts, which is often created as a result of outdated layouts. I like to refer to a lot of the traditional function-type layouts as farm layouts. As a farmer, you don't mix the planting of vegetables etc. together; you devote a section (row) of your garden to tomatoes; in another section or row, you plant corn; and so on. This is how many traditional (outdated) layouts are created; we group various pieces of the same equipment (i.e. same function) together and sometimes make it worse by putting a wall around them. We ignore the overall product flow throughout the end-to-end process; thus,

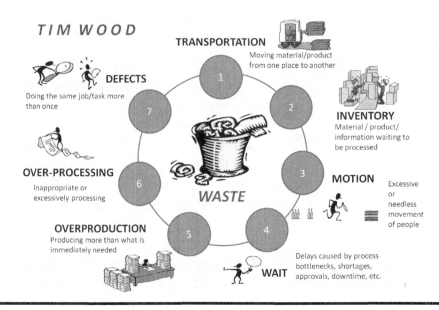

Figure 2.3   T-I-M-W-O-O-D: The seven categories of waste.

we are forced to transport product, materials etc. from function to function. Transportation waste can be caused by large batch sizes that require material to be moved on pallets or in large containers, totes, etc. It can also be created by mura (unevenness) or overproduction; we create inventory that must be transported because our production is not synchronized with consumption (demand).

To assess the amount of transportation waste that exists within a factory, a good visual tool is the spaghetti diagram. A spaghetti diagram is a visual representation of the product flow through a factory (or office) that uses a continuous flow line to trace the path of a product (or any item) through its process. Although I'm not sure of the origin of the phrase "spaghetti diagram", certainly when we draw a line representing an item's flow the result often ends up looking like a plate of tangled spaghetti.

Figure 2.4 shows an example of a very simple spaghetti diagram.

Another tool for assessing transportation waste is Routing By Walking Around, which was covered during the Assessment Tools and Methodologies section of this book.

The best solution for minimizing transportation waste is cellular manufacturing, i.e. converting your function-based (farm) layout to a process-based layout (cellular). The basic principle of cellular (process-based) manufacturing is that by grouping products with similar processes into a manufacturing cell of dedicated equipment, the sequentially arranged equipment will

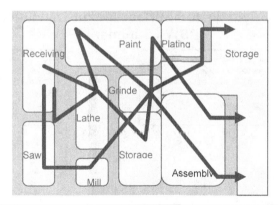

Figure 2.4   Example – Simple spaghetti diagram.

promote a continuous flow of the product and minimize transportation and handling. A U-shape is common for these cells; the operators are inside the "U" so that they can support multiple types of equipment and minimize walking (and transport) distances. Many companies interchange the terms *cell* and *line*.

Case-in-Point Example 2.3 Cellular Manufacturing (Transportation Waste Reduction)

I have multiple examples in regards to the elimination of transportation waste through cellular manufacturing. I'll use a simple representative example from a Fortune 100 company's semiconductor test and assembly operation. The existing layout was a traditional layout like the one I've previously described, with the equipment grouped by function: e.g. die attach, wire bonding, curing, molding, and testing. By using the RBWA to complete the assessment of the current layout, we revealed that 14% of the process steps were transportation and 12% of the process time was attributed to transportation. Converting the existing functional layout into a manufacturing cell reduced the transportation steps by 96% and the transportation time by 87%.

Graphs in Figure 2.5 represent the RBWA findings of the current state and the proposed future state.

Another opportunity to reduce transportation waste is the deployment of "Point-Of-Use Storage (POUS)" for raw material and/or subassembly deliveries to production. POUS can be accomplished by internal material handlers or external suppliers that deliver directly to POUS with their customers' manufacturing area. Now, this may sound like common sense, but it's actually a best-practice concept that is seldom deployed in most manufacturing environments.

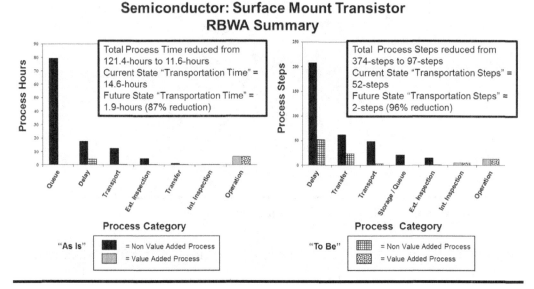

Figure 2.5   Case-in-Point Example 2.3 RBWA Analysis: Current vs. future states.

Case-in-Point Example 2.4 Point-Of-Use Storage (Transportation Waste Reduction)

This case story will simply be an example of a very effective implementation of Point-Of-Use Storage (POUS). The company in this example was an OEM manufacturer of industrial equipment. This company consumed hundreds of different types and sizes of mechanical hardware on a daily basis. Initially, the company developed kanbans (mostly max–min sizing) and utilized water-spiders, internally, to replenish kanbans located in supermarkets or production-side locations from a centralized raw material storage area. This is a fairly common approach, but then the company realized through various kaizens that this didn't really add any value. They already had a strong supplier relationship with a local hardware distributer/supplier. The supplier's staff was already fairly strong in their understanding of Lean concepts, so the OEM company held joint kaizen events with the supplier to devise a POUS replenishment scheme for most of their common hardware items to POUS locations (supermarkets and production-side workstations). The scheme went though some learning pains but quickly became a very effective concept. So, not only were thousands of transportation steps eliminated (centralized storage to POUS), but also, since the supplier was managing hundreds of hardware SKUs, the OEM company no longer had to. The supplier would provide a weekly invoice of the replenishment quantities to the company, which could reconcile the quantities with their weekly shipments (bill of materials). There were minor variances between shipment quantities and invoices, but these variances were within established acceptable limits; the allowable variances were based on A-B-C stratification of the hardware based on item costs. This was a highly successful program that saved the OEM company thousands of dollars in administrative and indirect labor (water-spiders) costs.

In case "water-spiders" are a new concept for you, it means a manufacturing material handler whose main task is to make sure material is supplied to POUS as needed so that other manufacturing associates can concentrate on their assigned tasks (assembly, test, etc.): i.e. value-added work. The water-spider may work to timed deliveries by location or respond to an andon or other replenishment signals.

Major transportation components of our supply chain or order fulfillment processes include the transportation of material from suppliers, the transportation of inventory to distribution centers, and the transportation of product to the customer. These types of transportation are most often value added; the transportation of items from a factory or warehouse to a distribution center could be perceived as non-value added, but I'm not going to debate the point here. But I do want to make the point that even though this transportation is value added in nature, it's highly probable that the overall transportation process contains a lot of waste. And this leads me to a very interesting case story in regards to "perceived" value-adding transportation.

Case-in-Point Example 2.5 The Frequent Flying Assembly (Transportation Waste)

One of the more interesting experiences that I've had with eliminating transportation involved a global integrated semiconductor manufacturer. They had a very complex semiconductor assembly that included multiple subassembly operations. The manufacturing process started with a wafer that was cut into dies; these were attached in semiconductor subassembly and then went through a second assembly and test operation before finally being assembled on a small printed circuit board assembly. This was a very high-volume product, so the company's goal was to maximize their profit margins on the product. Their purchasing, engineering, and production group formed a task force to pursue the cheapest possible sources for each (3) element of the assembly process. The wafer would be produced at its wafer foundry in Asia with the intent of outsourcing everything else (to its neighboring low-cost labor countries). After an extensive analysis of potential suppliers, quotes, and proposals, the task force found that the cheapest overall assembly price would be to procure the parts from three separate suppliers; the only issue was that they were located in three separate neighboring countries. So, they would have an assembly supply chain across four countries – all neighboring (although two were island nations) – but they justified the transportation cost as they would only utilize ground and sea transportation modes, and the assembly cost was so much cheaper than in the originating country. The total transportation process consisted of an initial ground transportation segment of 30 hours and about 1,500 miles; the second segment consisted of 10 hours and about 800 miles of ground transportation and another 4~6 days of sea transportation; the third segment was another 4~6 days of sea transportation and then 2 hours and about 60 miles of ground transportation; and then, finally, 2 hours and about 30 miles of ground transportation back to the company's finished goods warehouse (same physical location as the foundry). So, conservatively, there's about nine days of transportation within the assembly's total process lead time. But, based on the transportation cost estimates and the subassemblers' quotes, this was going to be a major financial windfall for the company, and the task force was highly praised for their effort. Champagne for all! Woo-hoo!

This assembly was proclaimed as one of the highest margin profit margin products within this Fortune 500 company's vast and diversified product portfolio.

A simple diagram of the production flow can be seen in Figure 2.6.

I was a lead consultant on a huge supply chain assessment/transformation project contracted by this company's US headquarters. As I was doing my initial analysis, this assembly immediately grabbed my attention (a Lean red flag!), as my 20+ years of experience (at that time) told me that there had to be a lot of waste in this fragmented supply chain. But I was assured that this process and its cost had surpassed intensive due diligence (and was ridiculed for thinking otherwise), and I was told I was wasting my time and their company's money (i.e. my consultancy fees). But to me, it was obvious that there was too much transportation and too many administrative activities in this

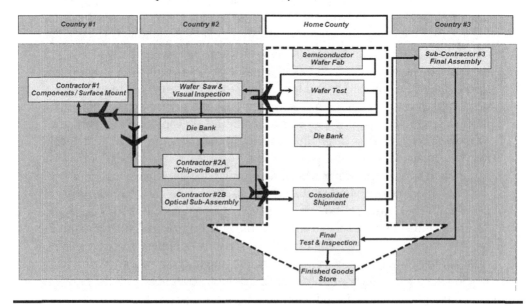

Figure 2.6   Case-in-Point Example 2.5 multi-country production flow diagram.

process to offset the sub-contracted labor activities. So, we start with nine days of transportation plus about ten days of WIP throughout the process and about two hours of value-added assembly and test: again, conservatively, a process lead time of 19 days. But as I started my cost analysis, I immediately found out that the company's cost structure treated logistics cost as an allocation, not as an actual cost. So, the cost figures for this assembly did not reflect the actual cost incurred. And when I looked at the actual transportation costs, I found that the ground–sea transportation scenario that I described earlier was not being followed, as almost all shipments were by air: not ground or sea, but air. Anyway, I became the whistle-blower on this situation, thus forcing the internal financial team to review the actual numbers; what had been proclaimed as the most profitable product in their portfolio was soon verified to be a huge financial loss, including a double-digit negative profit margin. Based on the findings of their finance team, the full assembly was outsourced to a single sub-contractor, and a respectable positive profit margin was quickly obtained. The total process lead time was reduced from 19 days to fewer than 5 days (including the sea transport).

T**I**MWOOD: *Inventory*

Inventory waste is any material or product that's on hand other than what's needed to satisfy immediate customer demand. Inventory may be in many forms such as raw material, work in process, finished goods, spare parts, consumables, supplies, documentation, etc.

Inventory is considered a waste as it can negatively affect your operational performance in several ways by:

■ increasing your process lead time (Little's Law);
■ tying up cash (creating more of a cash liability rather than an asset);
■ cost of money, i.e. interest paid on money used to purchase inventory or interest lost as money tied up in warehouse vs. in a bank gaining interest;
■ requiring extra resources; e.g. floor space (+ associated utilities), material handling;
■ hiding problems – you have probably seen a version of the "boat over rocks" illustration such as that in Figure 2.7.

In Figure 2.7, as a traditional process (our "boat") runs with too much inventory (the "water" in the illustration), forcing long process lead times because the process has no idea where the bottlenecks (the "rocks") are. Inventory can definitely give you a false sense of security, as it often takes the urgency out of doing everything right the first time. Inventory gives you

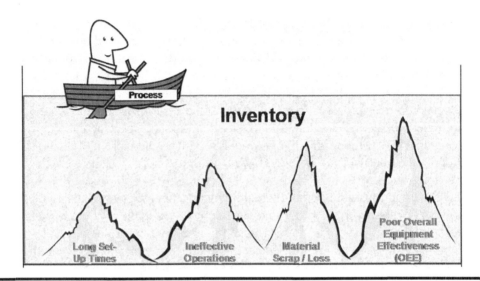

Figure 2.7   Inventory hides process issues/opportunities.

a buffer for your mistakes and does not require immediate countermeasures to fix. So, inventory allows you to continue along without immediately identifying and correcting the root causes of problems.

Inventory also allows you to be ineffective:

■ Equipment set-ups and/or product changeovers times are not as critical as you'll have buffer stock.
■ Inventory gives you a "safety" buffer (hopefully it'll be the right product … most of the time), but there will be long lead times: i.e. less responsiveness to changes in customer demand.
■ Poor quality can be offset by safety stock, just-in-case inventories … and overproduction.

Inventory can be a symptom of poor operational performance: i.e. inventory is the proverbial double-edged sword. Inventory covers your inefficiencies, but it's equally the result of other inefficiencies.

Inventory is created by (or is a symptom of):

■ mura (unevenness);
■ poor flow (material, product, information, and people);
■ production not synchronized with true customer demand;
■ large lot sizes (long set-ups/product changeover times, inspection/quality schemes, process bottlenecks, nothing more than being a legacy, etc.);
■ poor manufacturing run strategies (or lack thereof);

■ lack of Standard Work ... Standard Work-in-Process (WIP);
■ poor execution of inventory management practices (FIFO, cycle counts, A-B-C stratification, buffer stock sizing, just-in-case scenarios, etc.);
■ poor procurement practices (minimal or no strategy, minimal or no commodity differentiation, minimal or no strategic sourcing, minimal or no supplier relationship management, minimum order quantities, etc.).

So, how do we go about addressing this situation, i.e. waste of inventory?

The number one solution in managing and controlling inventory can be a "pull" scheme. A "pull" scheme simply allows your customers' demand to trigger your production activities: it synchronizes your operations. Customer demand can be external or internal. The "pull" scheme can become asynchronous and still be extremely effective and efficient by the strategic use of supermarkets (a decoupling technique).

The most important element of a synchronous or asynchronous "pull" system is the kanban/kanban system. Unless this is your very first foray into any aspect of Lean, I am sure that you're familiar with kanbans and some form of replenishment. But the one element of Lean that is often unsuccessful for many companies is the effective deployment of a kanban replenishment system. The reasons for these failures include:

■ not using statistical methodologies in determining the kanban sizes (standard deviation of demand and lead time, probability of a shortage, etc.);
■ not applying common sense; kanbans as part science/math and part art;
■ not having periodic reviews of demand, lead times (production and replenishment), supplier performance, quality levels, manufacturing and procurement intervals, etc.);
■ lack of discipline in execution;
■ poorly designed system (i.e. all of the above reasons).

Tools and methodologies that can be applied to control inventory waste include:

■ *SMED (Single-Minute Exchange of Dies)*: This is a process for changing over production equipment from one part number to another in as little time as possible. SMED refers to the target of reducing changeover times to a single digit; or a changeover thats less than ten minutes. This will be covered in detail in the "How To" section.

– I guess one misconception about reducing changeover times is that the priority is to improve OEE (overall equipment effectiveness), i.e. improved equipment availability, but the driving factor should be to decrease changeover times so that you can have more frequent changeovers. Your production runs can thus be more flexible (i.e. smaller lot sizes, more frequent product variations, etc.).

■ *One-piece flow*: Minimize the number of items being produced at a time ("one-piece" could refer to one piece of a product (preferred) or one lot/batch);

■ *Manufacturing run strategies*: e.g. Every Product Every Cycle/Interval, Rhythm wheel, A-B-C differentiation, etc.);

■ *Standard WIP*: Control the amount of material between workstations);

■ *Enterprise Lean*: Supply chain optimization (end-to-end synchronization);

■ *Strategic supply management*: Procurement, sourcing and supplier relationship management).

Case-in-Point Example 2.6 Cellular Manufacturing and Eliminating Inventory Waste (A Lean Transformation)

One of my early consulting projects was for a US Fortune 50 integrated semiconductor device manufacturer. Our initial assessment revealed:

■ very long process lead time (due to excessive WIP, i.e. Little's Law);
■ months of finished goods inventory;
■ large batch sizes;
■ a very conservative "build-to-forecast" philosophy; and.
■ a warehouse that was overflowing with just-in-case inventories.

The total supply chain process lead time (cash-to-cash cycle) for this product exceeded 250 days (wafer-fab to final test/assembly), which required a frozen customer order change window of one month. The existing manufacturing layout was a series of unconnected of process villages with a massive amount of WIP between "villages". The process lead time for the backend test and assembly operation was 10 days.

To reduce the process lead time, we had to reduce the WIP by several days; to decrease their responsiveness lead time, we had to create flexibility in production throughout the end-to-end's supply chain. The solution was the deployment of several key Lean concepts to create flexibility and responsiveness:

- reducing lot sizes by drastically shortening the product changeover times via the SMED methodology;
- strategic decoupling of internal supply by a creating a sub-process supermarket;
- replacing "process villages" with a cellular manufacturing layout; improving yield and product flow;
- creating a decoupling "supermarket" for an outsourced external process (plating).

We created a very efficient cellular manufacturing concept that drastically shortened the process lead time and thus improved the reliability of the supply of finished product; this would result in the elimination of just-in-case inventories. This allowed the company to shorten the frozen intervals for customer order changing, which not only increased customer satisfaction but also increased the company's competitiveness due to the fact that order lead time was a major factor in customer supplier-selection criteria.

The quantitative results were:

- lot sizes reduced by 67%;
- process lead time reduced from ten days to two days (and six months later was down to 12 hours);
- WIP reduced by 80%;
- lot size reduced by 67%;
- finished goods inventory reduced by 93%;
- customer's frozen order lead time reduced from one month to one week;
- annual savings projected to be greater than $1 million.

The reduction in process lead time and frozen order time was incorporated into a marketing video/initiative that highlighted the manufacturing changes achieved through this project.

TI*M*WOOD: Motion

Waste of motion is the excessive and/or inefficient movement of product, material, and/or information at a workstation, i.e. any motion not necessary for the successful execution of an activity. Waste of motion can also be linked to the ergonomics of the workstation.

Some examples of waste of motion include any twisting, stretching, or distorting of the body to reach an item, reaching for tools or supplies, searching for any item, loading or unloading equipment or containers (especially if a task could be automated or eliminated by new technology), and walking to get an item.

Waste of motion can be caused by:

■ poor layout of workstation (ignoring the principles of motion);
■ poor ergonomically designed workstations or equipment access;
■ processes that are developed without the operator in mind;
■ poor workplace organization (poor 5S – searching to find anything;
■ poor workplace layout (excessive walking, needing a step-stool or ladder to reach something, etc.).

Tools or methodologies to assist in minimizing or eliminating waste of motion include:

■ Standard Work – Combination Sheets, Time Observation Sheets, Job Element Breakdown Sheets, Standard Work Sheet, etc.;
■ workplace organization – 5S and visual controls;
■ RBWA assessment – opportunities to optimize motion, eliminate walking, eliminate or minimize lifting, etc.;
■ spaghetti diagram – minimize walking;
■ adhere to the principles of motion economy:
    – keep materials in front and close (~14 to 15-inches from the center of the body) (Figure 2.8);
    – arrange material and tools in sequence of use;
    – keep work at the proper ergonomic height;
    – locate materials at workstation so that they are easy to pick up;
    – keep body (trunk) motions to a minimum;
    – use gravity whenever possible instead of human muscle;

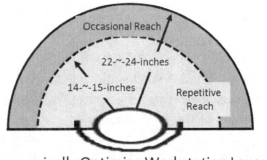

Ergonomically Optimize Workstation Layout

Figure 2.8   Principles of motion economy: Workstation layout.

- avoid zigzagging motions and quick direction changes;
- move with steady rhythms;
- if items are heavy and require lifting, use the appropriate lifting device;
- make handles and grips that are ergonomically correct in height and shape.

Case-in-Point Example 2.7 Eliminating Motion Waste: Offline Assembly

This example is for an OEM manufacturer that deployed straight, continuous-flow unit assembly lines (or cells); these assembly lines often resulted in a large amount of "motions" by the line-assemblers, as many workstations required a large variety of assembly components. These components were typically located in bins and racks, etc. behind the assemblers and required continuous body motions for retrieval. The constant torso turning of the assemblers also created poor ergonomic conditions and increasing fatigue (Figure 2.9).

The solution was to create modularized subassemblies that could be assembled offline and then quickly installed on the base units on the assembly line. A subassembly would consist of large number of components, and the workstations could be configured so that the components would be at optimized ergonomic positions surrounding the offline assemblers. The offline sub-assemblers would be working in a kanban supermarket replenishment mode, with assembly-line water-spiders keeping the online kanbans replenished. The workstations were less cluttered, requiring less motion, and were thus more efficient, increasing the productivity of each operator. This offline subassembly concept resulted in lower assembly lead times and lower costs/unit. The solution increased the number of operators but increased the throughput, lowering each workstation's cycle time. And the offline assembly workstation could support more than one unit-assembly line (Figure 2.10).

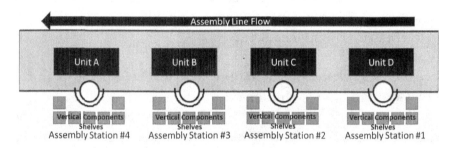

Figure 2.9   Case-in-Point Example 2.7 eliminating motion waste – Before improving.

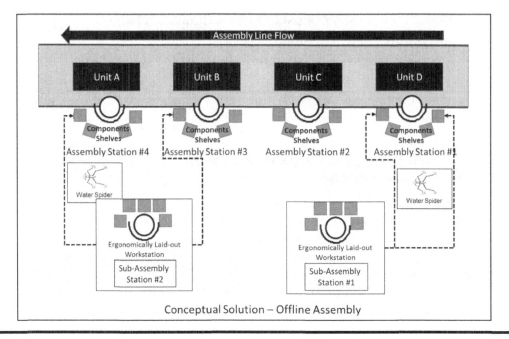

Figure 2.10 Case-in-Point Example 2.7 eliminating motion waste – After improving.

TIM<u>W</u>OOD: Waiting

Waiting is a delay (or ideal time) in a process that is created because information, material, people, equipment, etc. are not ready when they are needed. Waiting is often replaced by overproduction or busy-work to keep it invisible, and as a result waiting waste often creates other waste.

The waste of waiting can be attributed to multiple issues: large lot sizes, insufficient WIP, long changeovers, process bottlenecks, equipment availability, hand-offs/approvals, material shortages, poor layouts, outsourced processes, unbalanced production, etc.

The opponent of waiting is the presence of Flow … flow of material, flow of product, flow of information, and flow of people.

Ways to combat waiting include:

■ *Workload balancing*: Balancing the workload of operators in a cell so that waiting time is eliminated or minimized. Tools to be utilized to balance a work area include Value Stream Mapping, Operator Balancing Sheets, Standard Work Combination Sheets, and Yamazumi Charts.

■ *Standard Work*: Standard Work ensures that tasks are performed in the proper sequence and in the same way every time. Standard Work helps to minimize variations that can lead to waiting

■ *Decoupling*: It is often a far easier task to balance a work cell or line than to balance all elements of a process, especially in factories that are vertically integrated or have upstream or downstream processes with a wide range of cycle times. The key to the overall effectiveness of factory, in these situations, may be to decouple the upstream and downstream processes or operations. To decouple processes or operations, you may utilize kanbans and supermarkets. This creates an effective asynchronous pull system.

■ *Visual controls*: These can also help minimize or eliminate waiting by highlighting delays before they occur. Warning signs to potential disruptions to flow can be too much or too little WIP (e.g. empty kanban locations), empty or full document in/out baskets, low raw material levels (visual max–min controls), flashing andon lights, misses on hour-by-hour targets, etc.

Case-in-Point 2.8 Example Decoupling Processes (Eliminating Waiting)

For a highly vertically integrated OEM manufacturer, the only feasible way to eliminate or minimize waste of "waiting" was to decouple all upstream operations from downstream final assembly. This facility implemented electronic kanbans for basically all upstream and midstream operations. The facility manufactured thousands of different SKUs of upstream components and midstream sub-assemblies. The facility still operated via a pull system, but the supermarkets created an asynchronous system that decoupled upstream operations from downstream assembly, which operated in response to customer-order pull signals. The facility kept a minimal finished goods inventory but did maintain strategic finished goods inventory for a few customers who might request a lead time of a day or two for emergency orders.

Case-in-Point Example 2.9 Line Balancing – Yamazumi Chart (Eliminating Waiting)

An OEM manufacturer targeted an assembly line that was struggling to consistently meet their hour-by-hour takt rate chose to use a Yamazumi Board as a tool to assist in the redesigning of the assembly line. The redesign of the assembly line would be accomplished through a kaizen event, and this company had an established structure for their kaizen events. One of the

Created during a Kaizen & a Continuous Improvement tool; i.e. always striving to eliminate the "red" & "yellow" ; and shorten the "green".

Example of a "working" Yamazumi Board.

Figure 2.11 Working Yamazumi board.

first activities was to complete a detailed time study of all operations, with a detailed breakdown of all job elements. The initial observation revealed that the line was not balanced, and thus some operators had substantial wait times; it was decided a Yamazumi Chart should be created to better assess the situation. A Yamazumi Chart is constructed by stacking all the job elements of an operator against the targeted takt time. The job elements are scaled proportionally based on the elapsed time to complete the element. Each element is color-coded as green (value added), red (non-value added or pure waste), or yellow (non-value added but required). The Yamazumi Chart was constructed during the kaizen event with brown paper and colored magnetic strips, and the kaizen participants (line operators, line lead, supervisors, Lean team engineer and technician, etc.) were then able to maneuver the job element strips to optimize the balancing the operators' job elements (Figure 2.11).

But before proceeding with the balancing activities, the participants evaluated all the red (non-value added or pure waste) and yellow (non-value added but required) job elements to try to eliminate or minimize them. With some tooling and fixturing redesigning, it was determined that there were some elements that could be eliminated; additionally, it was determined that optimizing the layout of the workstations could remove some "motion" from other elements. After all elements have been optimized by eliminating and minimizing non-value-added segments, then the balancing of the operators and line could commence. The resultant of the kaizen was a balanced line (minimizing any waiting) that could meet the targeted takt time without adding any operators. The Yamazumi is maintained in the workplace, as the team would continuously seek to improve the operations by reducing the cycle time of the job elements and to eliminate and minimize non-value-added activities.

TIMWOOD: Overproduction

Overproduction is manufacturing more products than are immediately required by customers (internal and external), i.e. producing too much or producing before it is required.

The fact that Toyota considers "overproduction" as the worst of the original seven deadly wastes has often been cited, which is most likely because overproduction creates additional categories of waste. Clearly, overproduction creates excess inventory, which:

■ increases the volume of product, etc. to be transported;
■ increases lead time (think Little's Law), with excess inventory/lead time equating to larger number of defects (see section on "Defects" below);
■ equates to longer queues and lead times, i.e. waiting;
■ requires the utilization of resources before demand is realized, i.e. anti "just-in-time";
■ requires extra space;
■ equals over-processing, i.e. creating just-in-case inventories.

The causes of overproduction include:

■ just-in-case inventories – just in case it might be needed in the future;
■ equipment utilization – the traditional/old-school thinking was (is) that all equipment (especially high dollar capital expenditures) should be continuously run regardless of actual demand, as the goal was to maximize plant efficiency by producing large amounts of inventory throughout the manufacturing process. But Lean thinking is to synchronize production to actual customer demand and manufacture in a "just-in-time" mode, thus minimizing finished goods inventory (FGI);
■ long set-up and changeover times – overproduce to minimize set-ups and changeovers;
■ producing to a forecast – the "old" saying about forecast is you'll be either lucky or lousy (i.e. producing to a forecast is risky);
■ using up excess raw materials or subassemblies;
■ optimizing a segment of an enterprise and not looking at the end-to-end enterprise.

Case-in-Point Example 2.10 Driving the Wrong Behavior (Overproduction)

- A global telecommunication manufacturer's Key Performance Indicator (KPI) was plant efficiency, measured as total units produced/theoretical output capacity. This KPI is maximized by continuing to manufacture the product even if there's no direct demand for it. This is a case of a metric driving the wrong behavior, i.e. overproduction. This company often created a self-imposed month-end bullwhip, as they would ramp up at the end of the month to meet monthly metrics regardless of actual demand. It should be noted that years later this company was in bankruptcy status.
- A medical device manufacturer had a bottleneck piece of equipment (a bottleneck but not a constraint to takt rate or achieving customer demand); they had a strategy to manufacture and maintain a large quantity of buffer stock in front of the equipment to ensure that the equipment was never idled. The capacity of the equipment exceeded the actual demand/takt rate. This overproduction, obviously, led to excess inventory, waiting at bottleneck, and a longer process lead time.

Case-in-Point Example 2.11 Managing Capital Equipment (Overproduction)

A semiconductor assembly and test company wanted to ensure that their molding's cure ovens were always "full" for every cure cycle, i.e. that there was no unused space within the oven. The "Standard WIP" quantity in front of the cure ovens exceeded the loading capacity of the oven with no direct correlation to actual demand. The results were that the finished goods inventory was maintained at approximately 10 days of demand (about 20 manufacturing shifts of product output). In this case, the Lean solution was to create manufacturing cells that shared a curing oven; the curing ovens thus operated non-stop but were not always fully loaded to the maximum volume. The cells' output was equal to the actual customer tact rate, and the resulting output was a finished goods inventory of one day maximum. Product was shipped to customers daily (inventory turns > 300). Lot sizes were reduced from 3,000 devices to 1,000 devices. OEE of ovens dipped (90% to 72%), but inventory was reduced by 90% (cash flow improved by 90%, a $26 million reduction in FGI). The reduction of lot sizes increased the manufacturer's responsiveness to variations in customers' actual demand/mix, resulting in a huge increase in customer satisfaction (overall customer satisfaction rating by key customers from the mid-80s to upper 90s).

Case-in-Point Example 2.12 Every Product Every Interval (Overproduction)

A medical device manufacturer had model changeover times > 40 hours, so they purposely planned very large production-run cycles; i.e. Every Product Every Interval (EPEI) of four weeks, which resulted in large amounts of over-produced inventory (approximately six weeks of inventory). This overproduced inventory created significant levels of excess and obsolete products, resulting in large annual write-offs of C products (high-mix, low-volume products). A major SMED initiative reduced the changeover times by 60% and thus reduced the EPEI to less than two weeks. Average FGI was reduced from six weeks to two weeks (including statistically sized safety stock). With the reduced EPEI, increased demand flexibility resulted in on-time-in-full (OTIF) service level increasing from 93~96% range to > 98% for A products.

TIMWOOD: Over-Processing

Over-processing waste is created by overdesigning an item in such a way that it requires more resources than actually required. Over-processing is often caused by not understanding the needs of the customers.

Some examples of over-processing include:

■ having a process that's more complexed than required, e.g. automating a process that can be completed at the same or better cost and quality manually, repeating a step of a process just to make sure, etc.;
■ producing something to tighter specifications than required by the customers;
■ inspecting something to a tighter tolerance or Acceptable Quality Limit (or Level) than required;
■ process steps that do not add value to the customer and are not wanted by the customer;
■ carbon copy (i.e. "cc") many people on an email instead to only relevant recipients; hitting "reply all" to an email instead of sending only to relevant recipients.

Case-in-Point Example 2.13 Over-Processing (a Medical Device Manufacturer)

This case story involves an example of over-processing by a medical device manufacturer and is very commonly seen within medical device manufacturing companies. This example is for an Asian-based tier one supplier of medical disposable gloves that supplies gloves to a Fortune 500 healthcare services company. Medical devices supplied for US consumption are subject to incoming inspection by the FDA (Food and Drug Administration, an US government agency). The FDA inspects incoming shipment to an AQL (Acceptable Quality Level) of 4.0, i.e. 4% defective product is acceptable. Failure of FDA inspection can have severe results for a supplier and their customers, including 100% inspection of future shipments from the "failed" supplier. So, suppliers will internally inspect to an AQL of 1.5%, thus over-processing (and over-rejecting) product to increase the probability of acceptance by the FDA. Medical device manufacturers will often perform additional over-processing activities, i.e. 100% inspection and/or multiple inspections beyond their customer and/or FDA requirements ... doing anything beyond your customers' requirements is over-processing. To many, this may seem like a great form of customer service, but my actual experience shows that customers perceive this over-processing as a lack of confidence by their suppliers in their ability to consistently produce at the required quality levels (AQL 4.0) – thus the need for added operations and/or inspection to tighter standards.

Case-in-Point Example 2.14 Too Many Signatures (Over-Processing)

One day I was in the office of one of the management staff of an oil and gas client, and as we were chatting, he started processing some of the paperwork on his desk. One of the items was an asset disposal form. His "complaining" about having to sign the document made me want to "investigate" the situation.

My quick assessment of the document and the corresponding process determined:

- He was not really a stakeholder in this activity; the form required his signature simply because he held a management position. He added no value to the actual decision to dispose or not dispose of the said asset.
- When I questioned him about the asset to be disposed of, he had no knowledge of it; he was basically just a "rubber stamp" signatory with no interest in the asset.
- His was one of 19 signatures required. His was near the last (17 out of 19) of the signatures to be obtained, and this particular document had been in sign-off circulation for over one month already. Those 19 signatories were spread out in multiple facilities, separated by as many as 15 miles, causing an additional waste of transportation.

■ This particular asset was over 15 years old and had an original purchase value of less than $500. The processing costs of the 19 signatories would far exceed the original value of the asset (and its current recoverable scrap value was estimated to be less than $100).

Wow – such a waste of resources to process this item!

TIMWOOD: Defects

A defect can be defined as any product or service that does not meet customer requirements or reasonable expectations. So, a defect can be any cosmetic, functional, or dimensional nonconformity of a product to the customers' expectations. But a defect is also basically any mistake or error that occurs operationally, transactionally, or administratively.

Causes of defects include:

■ inferior process and/or equipment capabilities;
■ poor product design, i.e. lack of manufacturability, testability, or serviceability;
■ human error; human error itself doesn't actually cause defects, but defects are caused when a human doesn't follow Standard Work or operating procedures, or is not properly trained;
■ poorly maintained equipment or fixtures;
■ poor quality of incoming materials.

Tools and methodologies to prevent or minimize defects include:

■ clear and concise Standard Work and operating procedures;
  – visual controls;
■ operator empowerment – stop at defect is the ability to stop a production once a problem has been detected by the machine or the operator (andon cords);
■ data-driven and fact-based problem solving – identifying true root cause and implementing proper countermeasures;
  – utilizing the seven basic tools of quality and 5-Whys;

■ process failure mode and effect analysis (PFMEA) – allows you to (1) identify where the process may potentially fail, thus creating a defect; (2) brainstorm ways to prevent the defect from occurring; and, finally, (3) determine better techniques for detection if a defect cannot be prevented;

■ mistake- or error-proofing (a.k.a. poke-yoke) – an engineered method which makes it very difficult or impossible to produce a defective product; the method deployed does not require human assistance to prevent mistakes or errors (i.e. defects).

In our day-to-day lives, we experience many mistake-/error-proofing methods, especially with high-tech electronics connectors. These connectors are designed so that they can only be plugged in/connected one way: e.g. USB, HDMI, USB printer cables, external storage units, or basically any computer peripherals. Mistakes are eliminated by designing the connectors so that they can only be plugged in one way; human intervention is not required to ensure that they're properly plugged, as the design ensures that this is the case. Other examples of mistake-/error-proofing in our daily lives are gas pump nozzles (unleaded, diesel, or leaded), an automobile's dashboard warning lights, an automobile's seatbelt non-engagement buzzer (and warning light), the diagonally "cut" corner of your phone's SIM card, color-coding schemes, etc.

The same mistake-/error-proofing methodology so prevalent in our day-to-day lives can be applied to manufacturing (or transactional) processes. It is the creation of devices that either prevent the special causes that result in defects or inexpensively detect when a nonconformity has occurred. A mistake-/error-proofing device is any mechanism that either prevents a mistake from being made or makes the mistake obvious at a glance.

■ *Example of a simple poke-yoke technique in manufacturing*: Let's assume a scenario where we're automatically stamping and grinding a widget, the critical quality dimension of which was its thickness. The widget's nominal thickness was to be 0.200 inches, but it had an allowable range of any thickness equal to or less than 0.210 and equal to or greater than 0.190 inches.

A possible error-proofing (defect elimination) solution for this scenario is shown in Figure 2.12.

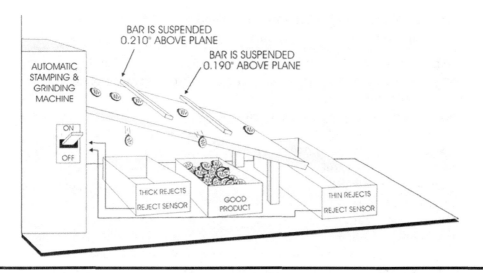

Figure 2.12   Example–Simple error-proofing (defect elimination) solution.

Case-in-Point Example 2.15 Process Integrity – IT (Mistake- or Error-Proofing)

Although I am not an Information Technology (IT) geek, one of my favorite mistake-/ error-proofing methodologies is the incorporation of process integrity into the IT system. Bar coding is a great enabler of this methodology. During my early years (circa 1983) in manufacturing, I had to set up a totally new surface-mount assembly department; since we were early pioneers in this area, we accomplished a lot by trial and error. The initial resultant was a fragmented manufacturing layout resulting in mountains of WIP and essentially no physical production control. And since we didn't know what we didn't know, we incorporated multiple inspection gates and multiple electronic testing stages into the processes. We were building millions of electric printed circuit boards a day in batch assembly and had minimal control of the lots within manufacturing. Our savior was that each lot was barcoded, and we had built the manufacturing process router into the IT system so it was able to 100% ensure that all lots went through all process steps in the proper sequence and that no failed lots could advance to the next operation. So, this closed-loop IT mistake-/error-proofing system brought 100% process integrity to a chaotic manufacturing environment. Now, I fairly quickly transformed this fragmented mess of a manufacturing layout into a cellular manufacturing scheme, and eventually it evolved into a single-piece flow process. But we retained the IT process integrity methodology by barcoding each printed circuit board assembly, which thus allowed us to run mixed products concurrently as the IT system ensured 100% conformance to the flow and that only "good" product could be advanced through the process.

Case-in-Point Example 2.16 Process Lead Time and Quality (Defect Waste)

I remember seeing the graph in Figure 2.13 early in my consulting career, and while it does somewhat make common sense after you ponder it for a while, I must admit that I was a little skeptical at first. What impact does a process's lead time have on defect creation?

Simply put, a shorter process lead time results in the product being exposed to potentially damaging elements for less time. Long process lead times are often the result of the other basic seven wastes: waiting/queuing, work-in-process (WIP), excessive product motion (handling), excessive transporting of product or materials, overproduction (inventory), etc. So, it does become common sense that the shorter the process lead time, the less opportunity for the creation of collateral quality issues. Additionally, long process lead times make a process more complex, resulting in any existing quality issues potentially being hidden (i.e. delayed detection). Thus, shorter process lead times equate to a shorter feedback cycle (i.e. a faster response time in the containment if quality issues exist). The reciprocal to the above scenarios is that a high level of quality will lead to shorter lead times, as there's less wasted time performing non-value-added activities: secondary inspections, rework, sorting, re-inspections, etc.

To add validation to this quality and lead time correlation, I'll share this case story. The company, a consulting client, was an integrated semi-conductor component assembly manufacturer, and the component in this case was a disk-drive head assembly. The client wanted to optimize their order fulfillment process. As with any improvement initiative, the first step was to establish a baseline of the current ways of working and the current performance metrics. Within this Asian facility, the total process lead time from the launch of a manufacturing work order to shipping the order out the door was 15 days; thus, this site kept a minimum of two weeks of inventory. The assembly first-pass functional yield was 86%; the

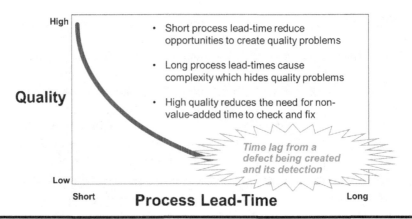

Figure 2.13 Impact of process lead time vs. quality.

failed units were manually adjusted until 100% passed. A critical part of the assembly process was a mechanical setting process (a setter), which controlled the functionality performance of the assembly, and then the assembly's "setting" was visually inspected twice (and typically manually adjusted repeatedly) prior to being submitted for the functional testing. The assembly and test lines were segregated by activities. All like-operations (functions) were grouped together, i.e. all "setters" grouped together, all "inspectors and re-setters" in another group of workstations, the "testers" in another group of workstations, etc. (hopefully you remember the farm layout reference from an earlier section). From our quick assessment (validated by conducting a Routing By Walking Around analysis and then creating a subsequent spaghetti diagram), it was obvious that our first step needed to be the creation of a series of manufacturing cells, as the current "functionalized" layout created continuous transportation of lots between functions and excessive motion by operators putting in-process assemblies into and taking them out of containers. Our cellular layout would eliminate transformation between functions and allow for the creation of single-piece flow of the assemblies between functions. So, each new manufacturing cell was inclusive of all functions from work order launch to final packing. The work orders were eventually eliminated as we went to a kanban pull system (with the replenishment signal coming directly from the customer in a neighboring Asian country). Additionally, we performed an assessment of the inspection/re-setting activities and found that very little value was added by the inspectors, so we instituted a "quality at the source" approach and had the "setters" inspect and re-set if needed; therefore, every piece passed on by the "setters" was good. And without changing the actual assembly and test operations, we increased the final functional test yield from 86 to 98%. These assemblies were fairly delicate, so the elimination of transportation and the minimization of handling improved the quality alone. The total process lead time to replenish the customer's kanban went from 15 days to one day (24 hours); the simple removal of non-value-added activities drastically reduced the lead time (93% reduction), resulting in a 14% improvement in functional yields, while the customer's out-of-box yield went from 98~99% to 100% (Figure 2.14).

Process Lead-Time	15-days	1-day
Final Inspection	100% Inspection	0% Inspection
Functional First Pass Yield	86%	98%
Out-of-Box Yield	98~99%	100%

Figure 2.14   Case-in-Point Example 2.16 results.

Chapter 3

Lean – Lean Building Blocks – How To

I will discuss a few of the "Lean building blocks" and I'll add a bit of "how-to" to assist you in your journey (Figure 3.1).

Flow

The importance of flow within a manufacturing environment was first recognized back in 1913 by Henry Ford at his Highland Park, Michigan facility. He had been producing his Ford cars for a few years when he realized that to reduce the cost, he need continuous-flow production. He was supposedly inspired by the continuous-flow production methods used by flour mills, breweries, canneries, etc. So, in 1913, he introduced his first continuous-flow assembly line. Although we always seem (and rightly so) to give a lot of credit to Toyota for pioneering Lean manufacturing, the truth is that Henry Ford was a pioneer in this area well before Toyota. And Ford hired Frederick W. Taylor (credited as the father of scientific management and industrial engineering, and one of the founders of motion and time studies) to help him identify inefficiencies in his operations. So, Henry Ford was looking to improve flow by removing waste and non-value-added activities in the early 1910s.

We must follow Henry Ford's (and Toyota's) lead and make flow a focus of our Lean efforts. So, for a Lean Transformation, we are concerned about

Lean Building Blocks			
Flow		Standards	Culture
Pull & Kanbans	Leveled Production	Standardized Work	Workplace Organization
Cellular Manufacturing	Single Minute Exchange of Die	Std. Mat'l Handling & Locations	Teams
Takt Time	Communication & Feedback	Visual Workplace	Training & Multi-Skilling
Flexible Capacity	One Piece Flow	Error Proofing	Job Rotation
		Total Productive Maint.	Total Quality Management
Continuous Elimination of Waste			
Supply Chain and Technology Integration			

Figure 3.1   The Lean building blocks.

the flow of product (or production), the flow of materials, the flow of information, and the flow of people.

The objective of flow production is to reduce product throughput time and improve productivity through the elimination of all forms of waste, i.e. muda, mura, and muri. The goal is to create an uninterrupted flow of product, materials, information, and people throughout the manufacturing or service-providing processes.

We can create flow production by eliminating or minimizing:

- *Transportation*: Optimize the proximity of equipment, warehouses, material, etc. to eliminate or minimize transportation of materials and/ or products.
- *Inventory*: Minimize all work-in-process inventories and optimize your Standard Work-in-Process (SWIP):
  - think "Little's Law": process lead time is equal to the total amount of WIP (work-in-process) inventory divided by the exit rate (Figure 3.2);
  - the less inventory, the smoother and faster the flow;
- *Motion*: Eliminate unnecessary movements and ensure the principles of motion are adhered to.

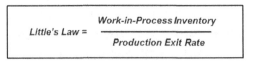

$$\text{Little's Law} = \frac{\textit{Work-in-Process Inventory}}{\textit{Production Exit Rate}}$$

Figure 3.2   Little's Law.

■ *Wait*: Eliminate waiting through:
  – workload balancing of operators and equipment;
  – Standard Work – minimize variations that lead to delays;
  – visual controls – proactively highlight delays.
■ *Overproduction*: Do not overproduce. Refer to Little's Law: inventory decreases your throughput velocity:
  – utilize Standard Work-in-Process (SWIP) to control amount of inventory allowed on the production line/cell and the amount of inventory allowed within the production area/workspace.
■ *Over-processing*: Simple over-processing steps can disrupt flow; e.g. too many approvals/signatures, too many hand-offs, excessive inspections, any just-in-case activities, etc.:
  – if it's not adding value to the customer, then eliminate it.
■ *Defects*: As previously discussed, long processing times contribute to the creation of defects and to deferred detection of real-time quality issues;
■ *Muri*: Don't overburden your people, equipment, or manufacturing cells:
  – overburdening disrupts flow: overburdening of associates may lead or contribute to increased fatigue or absenteeism; overburdening of equipment may lead to increased minor stoppages or increased downtime; overburdening of equipment can lead to a reduction of equipment performance.
■ *Mura*: Unevenness is the enemy of flow:
  – eliminate unevenness by balancing the manufacturing cells;
  – remove production unevenness with the aid of SWIP;
  – decouple operations with large differences in process lead times and/or cycle times using supermarkets;
  – utilize manufacturing run strategies and load-leveling methodologies (e.g. heijunka boards, kanbans, etc.) to smooth production.

The objective of flow production is to create continuous (non-stop) flow. Continuous flow is producing and moving one item at a time (or a small consistent batch of items) through a series of processing steps as continuously as possible, with each step making only what is requested by the next step.

Continuous flow can be realized in numerous ways:

■ one-piece or single-piece flow (remember a small lot or batch of items can be considered "one-piece");
■ moving assembly lines (automatically paced lines, motorized conveyors, etc.);
■ push-assembly lines (slide-lines); e.g. make one, move one.

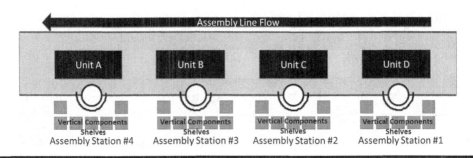

Figure 3.3   Continuous-flow assembly line.

Figure 3.3 shows an example of a continuous-flow assembly line (note: no inventory between units being assembled).

The most important type of information flow is the movement of information from a customer to the points where the information is needed (e.g. changes in customer demand, changes in purchase order (quantity or mix), customer complaints/feedback, any special request/instructions from the customer, etc.). Delays in the flow of customer information will invariably lead to poor customer satisfaction.

In addition to information flowing directly from the customers, there are many other types of information in a manufacturing or service environment, such as:

- kanban signals (kanban cads, electronic signals, email/fax, etc.);
- work orders (information to produce);
- production or lot travelers (information regarding a specific lot or batch of material or product);
- handover documents (material or product transfers);
- daily (or shiftly or weekly) production schedules, shipping schedules, etc.;
- companies with centralized customer service and/or a centralized sales and operation planning process may have a multitude of information flowing back and forth: e.g. demand forecasts, production schedules, daily (or weekly or hourly) shipping orders, and expedited information of changing conditions (demand, shipments, purchase orders, etc.).

Regardless of the type of information required by a service or manufacturing organization to deliver a service or product, the goal is the uninterrupted flow of any and all information.

Material flow is another key flow within a value stream. Material flow is the transportation of raw materials, pre-fabricated parts/components, purchased or assembled parts, manufactured components, final products, etc. Material flow can be accomplished through the use of:

■ motorized equipment (e.g. fork truck, etc.);
■ conveyors (e.g. motorized, roller, gravity-flow, etc.);
■ people (material handlers, water-spiders, associates, etc.).

Enablers of material flow include:

■ one- or single-piece flow;
■ SWIP – minimizes and control work-in-process inventories (back to Little's Law);
■ production decouplers; e.g. supermarkets, kanbans;
■ continuous production flow mechanisms (assembly lines, moving conveyors, etc.).

And a final flow that often gets ignored is people flow: again, the goal is interrupted flow.

Uninterrupted people flow can be enabled by:

■ job rotation and multi-skill training (a flexible workforce);
■ well organized and uncluttered workspaces (5S);
■ cellular manufacturing (e.g. U-shaped layouts);
■ optimized workspace layouts (spaghetti diagramming);
■ Standard Work compliance (Job Element Breakdown Sheet and Standard Work Sheet);
■ balanced manufacturing cells (Yamazumi).

A comprehensive tool to reflect on the flows of a value stream is the Value Stream Map.

Figure 3.4 shows an example of a Value Stream Map.

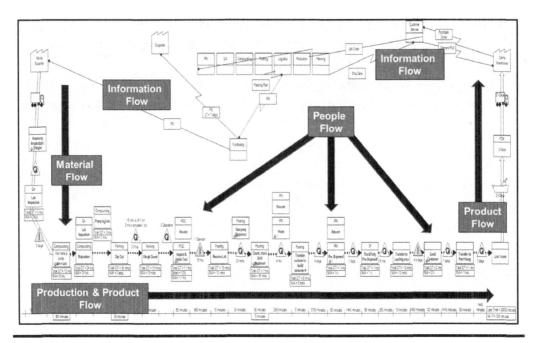

Figure 3.4 Value stream map example.

Case-in-Point Example 3.1 Continuous Flow, Trystorming, and TWI (an OEM Manufacturer)

This example is an OEM manufacturer with a manufacturing cell that continuously struggled to meet its takt time. The cell had an accurate hour-by-hour board and had regular tier meetings to address hour-by-hour misses, but the cell struggled in meeting its takt rate (completed units / hour).

A complete analysis of the manufacturing cell was executed utilizing a kaizen-created Yamazumi Board. The bottleneck was identified and more in-depth analysis was undertaken of that operation. A formal 3P was not initiated, but 3P principles were utilized to redesign the bottleneck workstation, including the 7-Ways and "trystorming" – and I would say a heavy dose of trystorming. Trystorming is a combination of brainstorming and rapid prototyping; designed to determine if ideas will work or not.

One of the issues with the bottleneck workstation was that an operator was required to access all sides on the unit being assembled. This required the operator to contort their body to get full access to the unit, plus it required walking over the conveyor to gain access to the back side of the unit. So, a new workstation design emerged that allowed the unit to be rotated 360° and be easily elevated/lowered as needed.

The final countermeasure, and the most important terms of "continuous flow", was the implementation of a motorized, continuous movement conveyor. The conveyor moved forward at a very slow continuous rate (unnoticeable at first glance) that set the pace for all operators (~6) along the line, at a pace that would ensure that the takt time would be met. A "pitch" was incorporated as the space for the unit being assembled plus a buffer space before and after; this pitch allowed an operator to recover if there were a minor slippage in their processing time.

The newly designed workstation required multiple operators to be trained on the operations (i.e. new Standard Work).

The training was conducted utilizing the TWI (Training Within Industry) principles, which were:

- instructor performs the task in silence;
- instructor shows trainee one cycle of work, pointing out the job elements;
- instructor shows trainee one cycle of work, pointing out job elements and critical points as they relate to safety, quality, productivity;
- instructor shows trainee one cycle of work, pointing out job elements and critical points as they relate to safety, quality, and productivity, and then explains why the critical points are important (i.e. critical);
- trainee performs the task for the instructor in silence;
- trainee shows the instructor one cycle of work, pointing out the job elements;
- trainee shows the instructor one cycle of work, pointing out job elements and critical points as they relate to safety, quality, and productivity;
- trainee shows the instructor one cycle of work, pointing out job elements and critical points as they relate to safety, quality, and productivity, and then explains why the critical points are important (i.e. critical).

After the training was completed (on all shifts), the cell's teams had no issues utilizing the newly paced motorized conveyor and the newly redesigned workstations and were consistently able to meet a new, higher takt rate (with no increase in operators).

Pull and Kanbans

Pull in a manufacturing, service, or administrative environment represents downstream activities signaling their needs to upstream activities. Downstream activities "pull" their needs from the upstream activities. Pull is the opposite of "push". In a "push" scenario, upstream activities would "push" their product, service, or information to the downstream activities without really understanding the needs of the downstream activities.

In a manufacturing environment, "pull" would most commonly be referred to as pull-production. Pull-production strives to eliminate overproduction and other wastes such as transportation, inventory, waiting, and defects. In pull-production, a downstream operation provides information (what's been consumed and at what quantity) to the upstream operation, often via a kanban signal. A kanban signal provides upstream activities with information about what part or material is needed, the quantity needed, and when and where it is needed. In a pull system, nothing is produced by the upstream supplying processes until the downstream processes signal a need. This is the opposite of push-production.

A common element of a pull-production system is a "supermarket". A "supermarket" in a manufacturing environment is a location where a predetermined amount of inventory is maintained to supply downstream processes. Each item in a supermarket has a specific location from which a material handler withdraws materials and/or products in the precise amounts needed by a downstream process. It operates similarly to your typical grocery supermarket: a "customer" (a downstream activity) takes what they need and then a "supplier" (an upstream activity) replenishes the supermarket. Actually, in the 1950s, Toyota developed their just-in-time system after analyzing and adopting the basic principles of the American fast-moving consumer-goods supermarket concept.

In a supermarket-based pull-production system, each process has a warehouse or store (supermarket) that holds a controlled amount of each product produced by that process. An upstream process simply produces to replenish what is consumed (or withdrawn) from its supermarket. Typically, as material is withdrawn from the supermarket by the downstream process, a kanban or another type of information will be sent upstream to authorize the upstream process to replenish what was withdrawn. The potential disadvantage of a supermarket system is that for it to operate at its highest efficiency, it must carry an inventory of all part numbers that the processes produces, which may not always seem feasible if the number of part numbers is large. To be effective, the strategy for a supermarket must link to a company's manufacturing run strategies (see Leveled Production), which would define manufacturing-replenishment intervals, manufacturing-replenishment lead times, etc.

Another form of pull-production is sequential-pull production, which is a pull system that utilizes a mechanism such a heijunka box (see Leveled Production) to assist in scheduling the replenishment of kanbans.

Most of my experience with pull-production has centered around a hybrid of the sequential-pull system and a pure supermarket. There's a decoupling of downstream customer demand from some upstream operations; once an external customer demand triggers the process by pulling its needs, that will trigger upstream activities. However, the activities will not be fully synchronized as the upstream replenishment processes may be sequentially scheduled in accordance with the upstream's manufacturing run strategies.

But we often have to decouple the system and utilize supermarkets. This is actually an asynchronous system, as many of the upstream parts will be manufactured at a different rate than customers' actual consumption. Upstream parts replenish production kanbans, but most often a customer order signals a withdrawal kanban, which is synchronous with the customer demand. However, while the pull signals to replenish the supermarkets are asynchronous, they are being pulled by the customers' demand (consumption) (Figure 3.5).

"Kanban" is defined as a signaling device that gives authorization and instructions for the production or withdrawal of items in a pull-production system. Kanbans have two functions in a production operation. They instruct processes to make products (a production or make kanban), and they instruct material handlers to withdraw or move products (a withdrawal or move kanban).

The most crucial element of a kanban is the sizing (quantity of material or product). You want to minimize stock-outs or unfulfilled demand while maintaining the bare minimum of inventory. There are many crucial factors that determine the size of a kanban, such as:

■ daily demand, historical or forecasted, is the starting point of any kanban sizing initiative;
■ manufacturing run strategies – intervals for manufacturing the replenishment requirements;

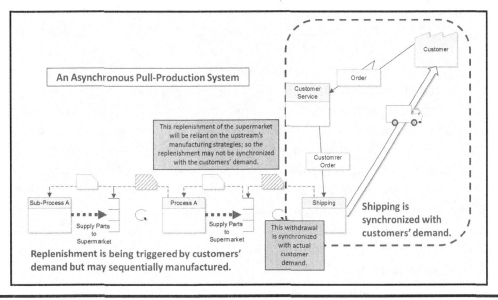

Figure 3.5 Example of an asynchronous pull system.

■ replenishment lead time – time required to get replenishment requirements;

■ service levels targets – what probability of a stock-out is acceptable (statistically determine the probability of a stock-out); this impacts the amount of safety or buffer stock to be included while sizing the kanban;

■ determining the amount of demand or supply variability that you compensate for in your calculation; the more variability that you want to compensate for, the larger the quantity of material required;

■ any adjustments to made for potential quality issues (supply quality or defects-induced);

■ economic order or manufacturing quantities – some suppliers have a minimal order quantity, and sometimes in manufacturing, you may a minimum quantity due to set-up times or base-material sizing (e.g. sheet metal blanks, etc.);

■ the actual number of containers within a kanban will be determined by the calculated quantity of items and the size and weight of the items.

There are several configurations of a kanban system:

■ The simplest form of a kanban system is a 2-bin kanban. A 2-bin system in a manufacturing environment would typically be executed by starting with two bins of materials, parts, or products, with a kanban card attached to each bin. The production team draws materials from one of the bins; once the bin is empty, the team sends a request for more materials, etc. to the warehouse. Either a kanban card attached to the bin or the bin itself would be used as a signal. Until the new (replenishment) materials arrive, the team relies on the second bin for materials if properly sized; production should never be idle.
  – One misconception is that a 2-bin system doesn't necessarily equate to two containers; a "bin" could consist of multiple containers. If a "bin" equaled three containers, a 2-bin system would start at six containers, and the replenishment signal would be activated when the third container is empty.

■ My favorite kanban configuration is the "K_{max}–K_{min}"; as the names implies, it is a max–min system. There are five components of a K_{max}–K_{min} system (basically the same as components for any kanban system):
  – **Demand (DMD)**
    • daily demand or usage, based on either history, forecast (backlog) or combination.

- **Process Lead Time (PLT)**
  - time from when a release (kanban card, work order, etc.) is sent to the manufacturing floor until parts are received (replenishment time);
  - for purchased items, this may be stated as lead time (LT).
- **Cycle Time Interval (CTI)**
  - represents the frequency (days) that a specific part is manufactured (i.e. manufacturing run strategy);
  - changing CTI allows trade-offs between transactions, capacity, and inventory;
  - if the item is purchased rather than manufactured, you would use order interval (OI) instead of CTI, which relates to the frequency that an item is ordered (purchased).
- **Safety Stock (SS)**
  - parts required to compensate for variation (i.e., demand, supply, quality, downtime, etc.);
  - based on the desired service level.
- **Trigger Point**
  - the inventory level at which a signal is identified to either make or buy more; it is typically at the K_{min} + Safety Stock level (Figure 3.6a,b).

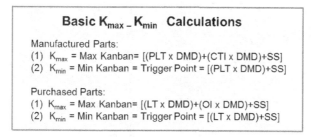

Basic K_{max} – K_{min} Calculations

Manufactured Parts:
(1) K_{max} = Max Kanban= [(PLT x DMD)+(CTI x DMD)+SS]
(2) K_{min} = Min Kanban = Trigger Point = [(PLT x DMD)+SS]

Purchased Parts:
(1) K_{max} = Max Kanban= [(LT x DMD)+(OI x DMD)+SS]
(2) K_{min} = Min Kanban = Trigger Point = [(LT x DMD)+SS]

K_{max} – K_{min} Kanban System

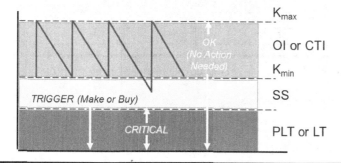

Figure 3.6 K_{max}–K_{min} calculation (top), K_{max}–K_{min} action levels (bottom).

The key to the K_{max}–K_{min} system (or any kanban system) is the safety stock calculation; that will probably be the difference between success or failure with your kanban system.

The most important factor in calculating the safety stock is identifying the desired (targeted) service level. The service factor that you use for your safety stock is statistically determined based on the chosen service level, i.e. the percentage of time where you will almost certainly have no stock-outs – 85%, 95%, 99%, 100%, etc. The higher the targeted percentage (service level), the larger the amount of required safety stock. The service level is essentially the number of standard deviations, relative to the mean, that should be carried as safety stock. It is literally the calculated number of times that you expect a stock-out to occur.

- **Service Level = 1** means that one standard deviation of safety stock is carried, and on average there will be no stock-outs 84% of the time, which would be a service factor of 0.99 (see Figure 3.7).

Service Level	Service Factor		Service Level	Service Factor
50.00%	0		90.00%	1.28
55.00%	0.13		91.00%	1.34
60.00%	0.25		92.00%	1.41
65.00%	0.39		93.00%	1.48
70.00%	0.52		94.00%	1.55
75.00%	0.67		95.00%	1.64
80.00%	0.84		96.00%	1.75
81.00%	0.88		97.00%	1.88
82.00%	0.92		98.00%	2.05
83.00%	0.95		99.00%	2.33
84.00%	0.99		99.50%	2.58
85.00%	1.04		99.60%	2.65
86.00%	1.08		99.70%	2.75
87.00%	1.13		99.80%	2.88
88.00%	1.17		99.90%	3.09
89.00%	1.23		99.99%	3.72

Figure 3.7   Targeted service levels & corresponding service factors.

$$\boxed{\text{Safety Stock} = \sigma \times \text{Service Level} \times (\text{PLT})^{\beta} \\ \text{where } \beta = 0.7}$$

Figure 3.8   Example safety stock calculation.

■ **Service Level = 2** means that two standard deviations of safety stock are carried, and on average there will be no stock-outs 98% of the time, which would be a service factor of 2.05 (Figure 3.7).

The factors for determining the safety stock (SS) calculation for a manufactured part would be:

■ demand variability (standard deviation: σ):
  – standard deviation for demand variability should be calculated as daily deviation for past the 12 months; a 12-month snapshot is best as it should capture any seasonality, etc.;
  – to calculate the demand standard deviation:
    • determine the average (mean) daily demand for given period (e.g. 1 -months);
    • for each daily demand quantity, subtract the mean (a above) and then square the result for each daily demand;
    • work out the mean of those squared daily demand differences (b above);
    • take the square root of that (c above) and you are done.
■ desired service level (stock-out coverage);
■ process lead time (PLT);
■ manufacturing on-time performance (β). Figure 3.8.

The alternative safety stock calculation, shown in Figure 3.9, is similar to the above formula but utilizes a calculated standard deviation for lead-time variations.

Alternative Safety Stock Calculation

<u>Demand Variation :</u>   <u>Lead-Time Variation :</u>
Safety Stock (SS) = Z x σ_D x LT   Safety Stock (SS) = Z x σ_{LT} x DD

If you have both demand & lead-time variations, and they're influenced by different factors

Demand & Lead-Time Variation (driven by different factors)

Safety Stock (SS) = Z x $\sqrt{(\sigma_D \times LT)^2 + (\sigma_{LT} \times DD)^2}$

If you have both demand & lead-time variations, and they're influenced by the same factors

Demand & Lead-Time Variation (driven by same factors)

Safety Stock (SS) = $[(Z \times \sigma_D \times LT) + (Z \times \sigma_{LT} \times DD)]$

Z – Service Level's Service Factor (see table above)

The Safety Stock component for purchased parts should include an incoming quality component.

- Uncertainty in demand results from:
    - Forecast error in the customer commit
- Safety stock to cover demand uncertainty is calculate SHOULD ed by

$$SS_{Demand} = Z \times \sigma_{DM} \times D_{avg} \times (LT)^{1/2} \qquad = 2.576 \times 50\% \times 1 \times (14)^{1/2} = 4.8 \text{ days}$$

- Uncertainty in supply results from:
    - Supplier on-time delivery
    - Incoming supplier quality

    Assuming these do not occur simultaneously: $\quad Total = \left((4.8)^2 + (1.9)^2\right)^{1/2} = 5.2 \text{ days}$

- Safety stock to cover supply uncertainty is calculated by

$$SS_{Supply} = Z \times \sigma_r \times D_{avg} \times (LT)^{1/2} \qquad = 2.576 \times 20\% \times 1 \times (14)^{1/2} = 1.9 \text{ days}$$

- Where

    Z = 2.576, the number of standard deviations from the mean that corresponds to a 99.5% customer service level
    σ_f = forecast error = standard deviation of commit forecast at full replenishment lead-time
    σ_r = reliability error = (1-(Supplier on-time delivery %)(Supplier incoming quality %))
    D_{avg} = average daily demand based on the previous month's actual demand (units/day)
    LT = full replenishment lead-time (days)

Figure 3.9   Safety stock calculation with demand & lead time variabilities (top). Purchased parts' safety stock calculation (bottom).

Case-in-Point Example 3.2 Supermarkets (an OEM Manufacturer)

The scenario for this case example is a vertically integrated OEM manufacturer. Their in-house operations included metal fabrication, electronic board assembly, component assembly (fabrication, welding, and painting), and final assembly and test. The diversity of these in-house activities results in a very large range of equipment cycle times and lead times throughout the facility. So, the most common methodology to decouple the various operations would be a supermarket, and the large degree of vertical integration required tiered supermarkets. The first tier of supermarkets would be for incoming raw materials or purchased assemblies; the second tier would decouple the metal fabrication and electronics assembly from the component assembly and the final assembly. The final tier of supermarkets would decouple the component assembly from final assembly and test.

All of these supermarkets were kanban- and pulled-based, but this company was most often caught running their factory from "hot boards" and "shortage lists"; the final assembly lines still experienced almost "daily" line stoppages due to material shortages.

The facility faced two major issues:

■ Because of the thousands of part numbers produced at this factory, scheduling was a challenge, especially in the metal-fabrication area, and there was no true (formal) differentiation of parts based on daily demand (i.e. no A-B-C stratification).

■ Safety stock was not statistically calculated but was more of a gut feeling situation; they tried to err on the high side, which may sound good, but having finite capacity (like most factories), they were making too many of some items while starving other kanbans.

The metal-fabrication area would be the largest challenge, based on the large number of part numbers (SKUs) and the large range of cycle times through the metal-fabrication area. The steps to developing a solution were as follows:

■ stratification of the metal fabrication parts based on daily demand (i.e. A-B-C stratification);

■ selection of "A"s as the first items;

■ some economic manufacturing quantities, largely due to utilization of the sheet metal sheets but also with some changeover time considerations;

■ determination of safety stock calculation based on daily demand and standard deviation of demand, process lead time and standard deviation of lead time, and finally, a service factor based on desired customer service level (~98%).

The result of the above activities was a robust K_{max}–K_{min} kanban-replenishment system for the metal fabrication activities, but the system was a sequential-pull system rather than a synchronized pull-production system. To effectively accomplish the required sequential-pull mechanics in the metal-fabrication area, the area's lead person would "schedule" the kanban make-slips (kanban make cards) utilizing a heijunka board based on the due date; additionally, the lead person would group the kanban make-slips to minimize changeover requirements.

This was an effective sequential-pull system because the A-B-C stratification resulted in differentiated replenishment lead times, which established later due dates for the Cs; this allowed the heijunka-board technique to be effective.

The overall result of the sequential-pull system was that reliance on "hot boards" and "shortage lists" was greatly lessened, and assembly line-stoppages were diminished due to metal fabrication shortages.

After the metal fabrication's sequential-pull solution was implemented, there remained another daunting manufacturing challenge, that of synchronizing the manufacturing and delivery of complex in-house core assemblies with the final assembly schedule. The core assemblies were basically make-to-order: when a customer order was received, an assembly work order would be released for the required part numbers and quantities. The solution was to decouple the manufacturing of core assemblies from the final assembly operations by creating mini-supermarkets for a couple of major core assembly areas; max–min inventories of mini-supermarkets were established based on historical daily demand. The result of the creation of mini-supermarkets and supporting replenishment processes was the elimination of the make-to-order scheduling, thus ensuring, at a high probability, the right part numbers and quantity of core assemblies were available when needed by the final assembly activities.

Case-in-Point Example 3.3 Kanbans and a Staging Supermarket (an OEM Manufacturer)

This case story involved a German manufacturing site in China. At this site, they manufacturer power-distribution products. The scenario that we faced was that their process involved a large fusion-type oven; it was imperative that this oven be fully loaded with a complete set of components each processing cycle. The components were a combination of mechanical and electro-mechanical parts that were machined and assembled in-house in a job-shop mode with widely varying cycle times. In the current situation, they relied on an ineffective, complex scheduling system which rarely produced the right quantity and/or mix of the right components at the right time. The company already had several sets of gravity-flow storage racks to store the machined parts and assemblies, and they laboriously try to monitor the inventory in the racks to provide the needed combinations of components for the fusion oven.

The good news was that there was a relatively small number of parts (less than 100).

The obvious solution was to implement a kanban replenishment system and to convert the gravity-flow-racks into a supermarket. So, the steps to implementing the solution were:

- gather the process-routing and cycle-time data on the various machine parts and the subsequent assemblies by executing a RBWA (Routing By Walking Around);
- calculate the kanban sizing based on daily demand, machining and assembly cycle times, and a small amount of safety/buffer stock;
- take into consideration limits on the quantity per kanban container due to some of the assemblies being heavy;
- determine the required part-mix to fulfill the fusion loading requirements and complete a A-B-C alignment accordingly;
- convert the flow-racks into a supermarket (pre-fusion oven). In the true sense of a supermarket, we dedicated rows of the racking to specific component part numbers and maximum / minimum quantities of kanban. The number of rows and number of kanbans varied greatly

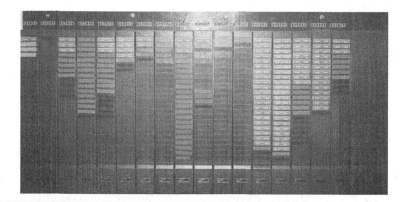

Figure 3.10   Example kanban board.

depending on the downstream demand, So, we developed a simple system to maintain a proper FIFO (first-in-first-out) flow;

■ create a kanban board to assist in managing the min–max scheme; kanban cards of consumed kanbans were located on the board until the proper number of kanban cards accumulated, thus signaling the correct quantity to launch a new production-make lot of those components.

An example of a kanban board is shown in Figure 3.10.

In Figure 3.10, the production launch occurred when all the "green" slots were filled with kanban cards; if you placed a kanban in the "yellow" slot, that was a warning, and if you made it to a "red" slot, then there was a risk of a component shortage, which would shut down the fusion oven and thus stop all downstream production.

This kanban supermarket scheme was a great success, eliminating unplanned idle time at the fusion oven, removing unevenness through the pre-oven activities, and eliminating the laborious scheduling activities. The divisional managing director praised my solution, particularly its simplicity and fit-for-purpose. I was later called back by the managing director to design a similar solution for a second China facility.

Leveled Production

"Leveled Production" is not terminology that I have used that much during my Lean career; it's a term that seems to carry multiple meanings (or interpretations). "Leveled Production" is often synonymous with production-leveling, which is also synonymous with production-smoothing (or heijunka in Japanese). All of these terminologies basically mean that the rate of production should remain constant irrespective of the fluctuation in demand. Its intent is to reduce mura (unevenness), which should minimize waste (muda).

But I've also heard "Leveled Production" referred to as pattern or repetitive production, and I think that that latter reference best relates to the methodology or concept that we want to deploy.

With "Leveled Production", we're wanting to create a repetitive sequence of what we manufacture, at what quantities and what frequency; i.e. a repetitive production-pattern. And I think in today's Lean world, we hear other terminologies that refer to the same concept:

■ Every Product Every Interval (EPEI) or Every Product Every Cycle (EPEC) or Every Product Every x (EPEx), where "x" could be any time interval (e.g. x days, x shifts, x weeks, or x whatever);
■ Production Wheel (a.k.a. Rhythm Wheel).

In my introduction to this concept, ~20 years ago, I was taught that this is a "manufacturing run strategy". And to me, that's what we're trying to accomplish: to establish a manufacturing run strategy that would remove unevenness from production and create a repetitive pull-production system.

But no matter what terminology that we use, the objective is the same. Basically, all manufacturing facilities have finite capacity and finite resources (people, space, raw materials, etc.), so it's important to make sure that a company is making the right quantity of the right product-mix at the right time.

The basis for any manufacturing run strategy should be a A-B-C stratification of the product portfolio (SKUs) based on historical customer demand.

I will start by discussing a manufacturing run strategy in simple terms: the deployment of an A-B-C strategy. This is a great application of an A-B-C stratification. Think vital or critical few versus the trivial many, and think of your *A*s being your critical/vital few and your *C*s being the trivial many; the *B*s fall in between but with a bias toward the trivial many. A reminder: A-B-C refers to the Pareto principle – $A = 20\%$ of the SKUs = 80% of the volume and $C = 80\%$ of the SKUs = 5% of the volume.

The main point is that you can't have a one-solution-fits-all methodology for production planning, production scheduling, and production execution, which is typically where traditional planning and scheduling processes fail.

Figure 3.11 shows an interpretation of a A-B-C manufacturing strategy (note that this introduces *D* into the stratification; *D*s are usually the real outliers with no foreseen demand but almost always get a random request here and there).

This can be translated into a manufacturing run strategy such as that in Figure 3.12.

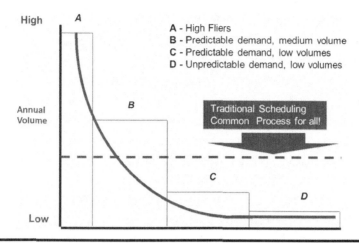

Figure 3.11   Differentiated manufacturing planning & scheduling.

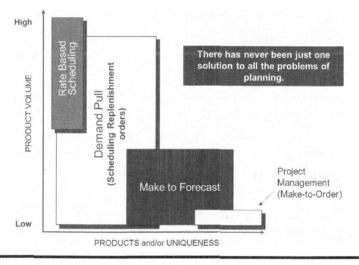

Figure 3.12   Potential manufacturing run strategies.

- *Rate-based scheduling*: Rate-based scheduling is considered continuous-flow production. It could also be converted into a Production Wheel / or an Every Product Every Day scenario. Basically, you'll want to manufacture your very highest-demand *A*s at a continuous steady rate every day (or every set interval: shift, day, week, month, etc.).
- *Demand pull* (scheduling replenishment orders): This is a demand-replenishment scheme where you're replenishing to a demand signal (kanban) but scheduling the actual production based on capacity. Typically, you would schedule the production replenishment again, such as Production Wheel / or an Every Product Every Interval (EPEI)

scheme with the interval daily or weekly. This is an overlapping category, as there may be some *A*s, *B*s, and even *C*s that you manufacture on a purely pull system. But the key here is that you based your pull signal (kanban) on different process lead time (a.k.a. replenishment lead time), and process lead time is based on the frequency (run strategy) that you produce your *A*s, *B*s, and *C*s. This is pull-production, and since the pull signals are very random, you'll often need to use a heijunka board to "schedule" your kanbans (heijunka is Japanese word that means leveling or levelization) (Figure 3.13).

■ *Make-to-forecast*: This is a technique that would be only used for the lowest-demand *C*s. For this category of *C*s, production can be forecasted and slotted into a Production Wheel or Every Product Every Interval, with the interval monthly, quarterly, or even yearly. You would seldom produce the *C*s, but when you did, you would build inventory to cover the historical demand over the "interval" period. This seems like it might be a lot of inventory, but remember, these are *C*s – i.e. low demand – so even a year's demand should be relatively small.

■ *Make-to-order* (a.k.a. project management): Because *D*s are classified as low volume with unpredictable demand, the holding of any inventory of a *D* product would be as high-risk, and *D* inventory would probably inevitably end up falling into an obsolescence or extreme slow-moving inventory category – not a desirable scenario.

A methodology that links well with above the manufacturing run strategies is the Rhythm Wheel.

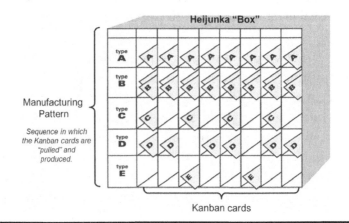

Figure 3.13 Example heijunka board.

Rhythm Wheel (a.k.a. Product or Production Wheel)

The Rhythm Wheel is a Lean scheduling tool for establishing a manufacturing run strategy and aligns nicely with A-B-C stratification. A Rhythm Wheel can be set up to run *A*s daily, *B*s weekly or monthly, and *C*s monthly or quarterly or whatever; any non-planned activity (*D*s) would be treated as an "event", and the Rhythm Wheel will have allotted time for planned events (unplanned events are not allowed) (Figure 3.14).

The basic principles of a Rhythm Wheel are as follows:

■ Inventory level (or kanban) replenishment is scheduled by the Rhythm Wheel and leveled across a manufacturing cell or production equipment (a heijunka board or box can be used to accomplish the desired leveling).
■ The Rhythm Wheel doesn't schedule exact SKUs, but it "reserves" manufacturing slots for *A-B-C*s; the actual SKUs that would be manufactured in that slot would be determined by a repetitive allocated slot (rate-based scheduling), kanban cards, and, most likely, some type of heijunka system.
■ A strict repetitive production sequence and a repetitive production cycle ease production, buffer demand volatility, and lead to a shortened learning curve.
■ The pull-mode avoids over- or underproduction due to forecast errors as the production is triggered only by actual demand (or kanban signal).
■ With the Rhythm Wheel concept, both leveled capacity utilization and low inventory levels can be achieved at the same time.

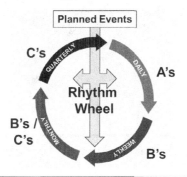

Figure 3.14   Example rhythm wheel.

The key benefits of the Rhythm Wheel are as follows:

■ Products are always scheduled in the optimal sequence. This leads to lowest possible changeover times and allows setting free capacity, which can create flexibility to meet changes in customer demand.
■ The repetitive production sequence leads to learning effects in change-overs, which in turn reduce changeover times further and improve the OEE (overall equipment effectiveness) of the manufacturing cell or equipment.
■ The fixed (standard) production interval, namely the Rhythm Wheel cycle length, leads to constant capacity utilization and transparent production schedules. This in turn allows a reduction of invento-ries and a better planning of supply from the upstream production processes.
■ The Rhythm Wheel minimizes scheduling effort by applying the pull principle and leads to less firefighting due to forecast errors.

Figure 3.15 provides an example of how a Rhythm Wheel can possibly be structured for a manufacturing cell or facility.

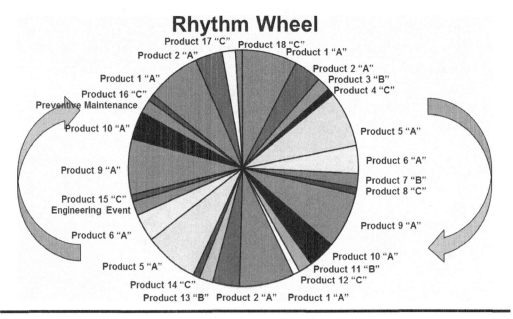

Figure 3.15 Example of a potential rhythm wheel configuration.

Case-in-Point Example 3.4 Manufacturing Run Strategy (Medical Device Manufacturer)

This case example involves a medical device manufacturer. This company produced medical gloves, which were produced on a continuous flow dipping line. A dipline could be equipped with approximately 4,000 to 10,000 molds per side; there was a left-hand side and a right-hand side. Typically, there was an offering of eight sizes, from 5½ to 9.

An A-B-C stratification of the eight sizes would reveal that the smallest and the largest sizes would be lowest-demand C-types, the second smallest and largest sizes B-types, and the middle four sizes A-types. The A-B-C stratification doesn't follow your normal 80/20 distribution because of the small population (8), but the four middle sizes are approximately 80% of the customers' demand.

The traditional manufacturing strategy was to run one size at a time and to have very long process runs, as the dipline changeover could be as long as 48 hours. This strategy would create large inventories of the four outlying (small and large) sizes. After much experimentation and some equipment modifications, it was determined that four sizes could be run concurrently, typically two As, one B, and one C on each side of the dipping-line; the percent of molds dedicated to the Bs and Cs would be very small. The ratio of the four sizes would closely follow the ratio of customer demand.

So, the manufacturing run strategy changed from loading basically one size at a time to concurrently processing four sizes at a time; this would reduce four changeovers for four sizes to no changeovers for four sizes, and excess inventory would be basically eliminated. To run eight sizes, it would still require a changeover, but to run the full range of eight sizes would require one changeover rather than eight changeovers for the original, traditional strategy.

Case-in-Point Example 3.5 Rhythm Wheel in Wafer Fab (Semiconductor Wafer Fab)

This case story involves a semiconductor wafer fab operation of a diversified global integrated semiconductor company. The site for this case story produced a large portfolio of semiconductor wafers. A typical high-demand wafer went through 22 major process (equipment) steps with a total average process lead time of 14.2 days. All of the wafers had varying process cycle times and shared many pieces of processing equipment.

It was determined that by setting up a Rhythm Wheel with a seven-day wafer-launch repeating cycle, the process lead time could be reduced from 14.2 days to an average of 6.5 days. A "virtual" cell was created by dedicating 40% of the site's equipment to its highest running product group.

To assess the overall process flow of this wafer group, a detailed Routing By Walking Around (RBWA) was conducted. The RBWA revealed that a typical wafer took a total of 1,977 steps (total tasks, not just equipment

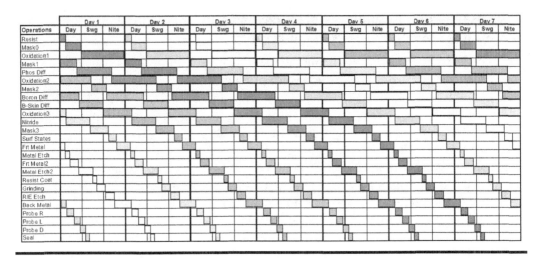

Figure 3.16   Example of a 7-day rhythm wheel pattern.

process steps) to complete, and the value-added number of steps was a very respectable 12%. With the implementation of the virtual cells, the total number of process steps (tasks) was reduced to 1,028, a 48% reduction. The value-added content was improved from 12% to 23%, a 92% improvement.

Figure 3.16 is a representative structuring of a seven-day Rhythm Wheel cycle launching a new lot (batch) of wafers daily on a repetitive A-B-C pattern.

Cellular Manufacturing

Cellular manufacturing is having a set of dedicated manufacturing resources "reserved" for a group of products that have the same (or similar) manufacturing sequences.

Some characteristics of an efficient and effective manufacturing cell are:

■ A manufacturing cell is a work unit larger than an individual machine or workstation but smaller than a traditional department.
■ An ideal manufacturing cell manufactures a narrow range of highly similar products and is self-contained with all necessary equipment and resources.
■ Cellular layouts organize functions around a product or a narrow range of similar products. Materials sit in an initial queue (preferably a kanban) when they enter the manufacturing cell.
  - Once processing begins, the product moves directly from operation to operation (or sits in mini-queues, a.k.a. Standard WIP). The result is uninterrupted flow of material, production, information, and

people. Communication is easy since every operator is close to the others. This improves quality and flow. Proximity and a common mission enhance the cell's teamwork.

■ Simplicity is an underlying theme throughout cellular design, e.g. simplicity of material flow. Scheduling, supervision, and many other support processes also reflect this underlying simplicity.

Case-in-Point Example 3.6 Cellular Manufacturing (Semiconductor Assembly and Test Facility in Asia)

This case story is part of a major Lean Transformation project for a global integrated device manufacturer. Our initial assessment revealed that long process lead times and high inventory levels were prominent throughout one of their backend semiconductor assembly and test facilities in SE Asia.

We chose one of their highest volume telecommunication components (a surface-mount transistor) as the product to drill down on. The baseline metrics were:

- process lead time = 10 days;
- lot size = 3,000 pieces;
- finished goods inventory > 4 weeks.

The solution was to implement cellular manufacturing. The existing layout was a very traditional functional layout that had similar equipment – probes, wafer-mount, visual inspection, die-attach, wire-bond, marking, molding, etc. – grouped together in the facility. I often refer to this as a farm layout – all the same vegetables are planted on the same rows, same area of the garden, etc. – which is great for a farm but inefficient for a manufacturer. This is, also, often referred to as "Process Villages".

Cellular manufacturing was our primary focus of this transformation; i.e.:

- Cell configuration and re-layout: To simplify product movement and minimize material handling.

But we, also, incorporated other Lean concepts including:

- Process analysis/RBWA: Identify and minimize non-value-added activities; reduce cure time, plate time, change to chemical de-flash and eliminate/minimize inspection;
- Process control and quality improvement: Root cause and establish control to prevent defects (poke-yoke);
- Machine set-up (SMED): Parallelize activities which can be undertaken while machines are running and increase production flexibility;

- Manufacturing run strategy: Categorize product groups building daily, weekly, and monthly to optimize machine conversions;
- Capacity, line balancing, and resource allocation: Allocate machine and balance operational capacity per demand (takt time);
- Kanban implementation: Control inventory and to synchronize production to actual demand; and
- Traceability and administrative support: To minimize non-value-added administrative support.

Our final solution had multiple cells with mostly identical equipment included in each cell. But since molding involves a huge mold press, this became shared equipment for all cells within that product family (one mold press for four cells). Process steps and travel distances were both reduced by 52%. And we reduced the lot size from 3,000 devices to 1,000.

The resulting metrics were:

- process lead time = 1.2 days (eventually reduced to < 12 hours);
- lot size = 1,000 pieces;
- finished goods inventory < 1 day;
- projected overall savings = US$2 -million.

Case-in-Point Example 3.7 Cellular Manufacturing (Computer Hard-Disk Manufacturer)

This case example is part of a major Lean Transformation project for a global integrated hard-disk component manufacturer. The transformation was a directive from their primary customer, who thought their lead times were too long and their out-of-box yields too low. This case example specifically deals with the company's backend semiconductor assembly and test facilities in SE Asia.

The initial assessment was an in-depth RBWA, which highlighted multiple improvement opportunities, but it was obvious that the main focus should be cellular manufacturing. The facility was laid out in a traditional-style, grouping like-equipment together with total disregard for product flow. A spaghetti diagram highlighted huge distances traveled by product, often crisscrossing its own path. The site had multiple end-customers, but there was no dedication of lines/workstations or equipment, which resulted in huge amounts of work-in-process inventories.

Our assessment also revealed that the excessive handling of product resulted in higher quality defects (this was validated with a controlled lot study).

We implemented:

- demand-pull system (fax-kanbans with customer);
- cellular manufacturing;
- one-piece flow vs. large-batch sizes.

The results were:

- total process lead time reduced from 15 days to < 24 hours;
- 14% improvement in first-pass manufacturing/test yield;
- 100% improvement in labor productivity;
- 18% improvement in line utilization;
- US$2.5 million reduction in WIP inventory;
- 12% improvement in out-of-box yield at customer's site;
- annualized savings > US$1 million;
- customer order fulfillment time reduced from two weeks to 24 hours;
- overall increased productivity at this factory led to a second Asian facility being shut down.

Single-Minute Exchange of Dies (SMED)

SMED (Single-Minute Exchange of Dies) is a methodology for dramatically reducing the time it takes to complete an equipment changeover (or set-up). The essence of the SMED system is to convert as many changeover steps as possible to "external" steps (performed while the equipment is running) and to simplify and streamline the remaining "internal" steps (steps performed while the equipment is stopped) (Figure 3.17).

Dr. Shigeo Shingo (of Toyota fame) is credited as the father of SMED, having developed the methodology in the late 1950s. The methodology isn't about reducing an equipment changeover to less than one minute; it's about reducing the changeover to a single digit (< 10 minutes). One of Shigeo's many claims to fame was circa 1970, when he cut the set-up time of a 3,000-ton sheet metal stamping press from four hours to three minutes. This feat didn't happen in a single step but was the result of continuously improving the changeover (over many months) until he reached three minutes.

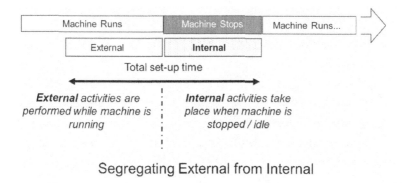

Segregating External from Internal

Figure 3.17   Segregating external & internal.

There is varying documentation of the number of steps for completing a SMED, from four to eight. Shingo originally spoke/wrote of eight steps:

1. Separate internal from external set-up operations;
2. Convert internal to external set-up;
3. Standardize function, not shape;
4. Use functional clamps or eliminate fasteners altogether;
5. Use intermediate jigs;
6. Adopt parallel operations;
7. Eliminate adjustments;
8. Mechanization.

But more important is that Shingo recognized FOUR conceptual elements, and these are the basics of the methodology.

1. Ensure that external set-up actions are performed while the machine is still running;
2. Separate external and internal set-up actions, ensure that the parts all function, and implement efficient ways of transporting the die and other parts;
3. Convert internal set-up actions to external;
4. Improve all set-up actions (remove all waste).

And it's the four conceptual elements that should be the backbone of any SMED system. Steps 3–8 of Shingo's eight SMED steps are improvement techniques, not necessarily steps to formalizing a SMED system.

Below are the seven steps that I recommend for developing (or deploying) SMED methodology:

1. Observe the current ways (a.k.a. current methodology):
   a. Videoing the changeover for detail analyzing later is recommended.
2. Separate the INTERNAL and EXTERNAL activities. Internal activities are those that can only be performed when the process is stopped, while external activities can be done while the last batch is being produced, or once the next batch has started. For example, go and get the required tools for the job BEFORE the machine stops.
3. Convert (wherever possible) internal activities into external ones (preheating of molds is a good example of this).

4. Streamline the remaining internal activities by simplifying them. This is where Shingo's improvement techniques (steps 3–8) come into play:
   – Use functional clamps or eliminate fasteners altogether;
   – Use intermediate jigs;
   – Adopt parallel operations (concurrent activities with multiple operators);
   – Eliminate (or minimize) adjustments;
   – Mechanization – the process of changing from working largely or exclusively by hand to doing that work with machinery (hydraulics, pneumatics, compressed air, etc.).
5. Streamline the external activities so that they are of a similar scale to the internal ones.
6. Document the new procedure and actions that are yet to be completed.
7. Do it all again: For each iteration of the above process, a 40% improvement in set-up times should be expected, so it may take several iterations to cross the ten-minute line (Figure 3.18a–c).

When analyzing your current changeover methodology, look for these improvement opportunities:

1. Shortages, mistakes, and inadequate verification of equipment causing delays can be avoided by check tables, especially visual ones, and pre-set-up on an intermediary jig;
2. Optimization for least work as opposed to least delay (simplification);
3. Unheated molds, which require several wasted "tests" before they reach the temperature to work;
4. Using slow precise adjustment equipment for the large coarse part of adjustment;
5. Lack of visual lines or benchmarks for part placement on the equipment;
6. Lack of functional standardization – standardization of only the parts necessary for set-up e.g. all bolts use same size spanner, die grip points are in the same place on all dies;
7. Too much operator movement around the equipment during set-up (TIMWOOD … M = motion);
8. More attachment points than actually required for the forces to be constrained;
9. Attachment points that take more than one turn to fasten:
   – Shigeo observed that it's only the last turn of a bolt that tightens it – the rest is just movement;

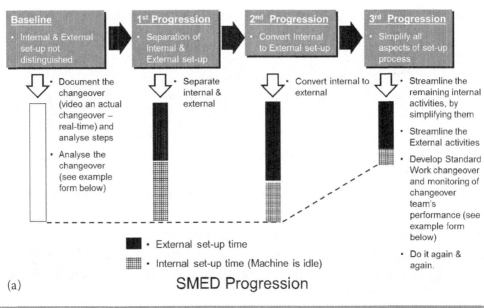

(a) SMED Progression

(b) Example of a Changeover Reduction Analysis Sheet

Figure 3.18   (a) Set-up reduction stages, (b) set-up reduction analysis sheet, (c) set-up standard work.

10. Any adjustments after initial set-up;
11. Any use of experts during set-up (standardization and simplification should eliminate the need for experts);
12. Any adjustments of assisting tools such as guides or switches.

EQUIPMENT CHANGEOVER STANDARD WORK & PERFORMANCE MONITORING

STANDARD CHANGEOVER ACTIVITIES					Process: _____ Area: _____
Item no.	Activity	External Time (min.)	Internal Time (min.)	Remarks/Key points	
					Photo or Visual Aids
Total Changeover Time (Min.)					

Required Tools: Required Personal Protection Equipment:

CHANGEOVER PERFORMANCE MONITORING

Change over no.	Date	Start Time	End Time	Total Int. time	Performed by	Remarks/Corrective Action	Acknowledged
Note: If total time exceeds the standard internal time of set-up, need to perform root cause analysis.							

(c) Example of an Equipment Changeover Standard Work & Performance Monitoring Sheet

Figure 3.18   Continued

Case-in-Point Example 3.8 Where Are You? (an Oil and Gas SMED Example)

This is a short case story and maybe not a lot to be learned, but I still thought it worth sharing.

The scenario involves an oil and gas company during one of the price booming periods (circa 2007) when oil was $140+/barrel. Additionally, this company was putting a huge focus on its Lean effort. They had just hired a new regional Operational Excellence leader, and one of the key initiatives was to shorten the process lead time for converting a freshly drilled well to a revenue-producing well, and this was referred to as a "well" completion to first-oil (C2FO).

Based on the past 12 months, the C2FO was averaging greater than 50 days, with an industry average that was probably 10 days or less. So, to really kick off an C2FO initiative with a bang, it was decided to film the changeover process for an offshore oil well. There had been some preliminary work done, so it was hoped that this changeover could be accomplished within a reasonable process lead time.

There were several critical path activities within the C2FO process; the first one would be the removal of the drilling wellhead and the placement of the pumping wellhead. This required a crane to hoist the wellheads for the removal of old and the placement of new. The targeted well was on an oil rig did not have a crane installed on its deck, so a crane had to be brought to the offshore site on a barge pulled by a tugboat.

So, the changeover activity was precisely planned; the Regional VP of Operational Excellence and some other dignitaries within the company would be on a nearby boat to observe and film the changeover.

So, in the early morning hours on the planned changeover day, everyone was in place, awaiting the arrival of the tug and barge. And everyone kept waiting; after four hours, the tug and barge still had not arrived.

A lesson learned:

■ The SMED approach should have been applied; the crane should have been at the rig before (as) the well was completed. Crane–barge logistics should be an external activity.

Case-in-Point Example 3.9 21 vs. 3 (SMED Standardization)

The scenario for this example is similar to the previous one; we're looking at the conversion of an offshore well from non-revenue to revenue-producing (the C2FO process). I was consulted to conduct an assessment of the total well C2FO process, and I had a target to drastically reduce the lead time from well-drilling completion to producing the first-oil (i.e. revenue). I reviewed historical changeover data from the previous 12 months and pareto of the causes of the delays. One of the top causes of C2FO delays was "missing hardware"; the number one item that was missing was a flange bolt. My investigation revealed that a typical pump wellhead had 21 variations of flange bolts. We rounded up all 21 bolts and laid them side by side; it was difficult to visually notice the differences in the bolts. There were differences, of course, such as a millimeter in diameter and maybe a few millimeters in length, but no huge differences. And after a technical / engineering review of the bolts, it was revealed that the 21 could be reduced to three, with no impact on the structurability or functionality of the wellhead.

This case story doesn't reference SMED directly, but it does reflect one of its principles, standardization; it was my changeover analysis that revealed the issue and cause. And since one of the major causes of long changeovers was missing parts, an 85% reduction in the number of SKUs required for the wellhead's installation will definitely lessen the opportunities for missing parts.

Case-in-Point Example 3.10 Attachment Points (SMED)

This case story involves a continuous-process dipping-line; the product being formed on this line was latex medical gloves. To change over the equipment (a.k.a. dipline) between different products required changing a "cam"; the cam was a large mechanical device that alters the molds (a.k.a. formers) dipping dwell time and entry/exit angles. It was attached to frame of the dipline by 40+ bolts and took approximately four hours to install or uninstall. After examination of the cam and the attachment to the dipline's frame, it was determined by a mechanical engineer that over half of the bolts could be eliminated as they provided no structural benefit. Thus, approximately 20 bolts were eliminated and the install/uninstall time was reduced to two hours, an easy 50% reduction.

Case-in-Point Example 3.11 External vs. Internal (SMED)

The scenario for this case story was a painting line for an appliance manufacturer. The painting line was a continuously moving line that utilized hanging fixtures to hold various parts (doors, side panels, etc.) for cleaning, preparation, painting, and drying/curing. The fixtures varied based on the part that it was "holding" during the continuous painting process. To change out the fixtures, the line had to be stopped and multiple fixtures changed at a time; the average line stoppage for fixture changeover was four hours.

As always, we had a target of 40% reduction in changeover time, i.e. from four hours to 2.4 hours. The current state was that all four hours were internal time. It was determined that the fixtures (with a minor modification) could actually be changed over while the line was continuing to move, So, the line never needed to stop to change the fixtures out. The line still had to be stopped for about five minutes to change color and flush out the spray lines. The net improvement in changeover time was 96%.

Figure 3.19 shows some typical SMED improvement techniques.

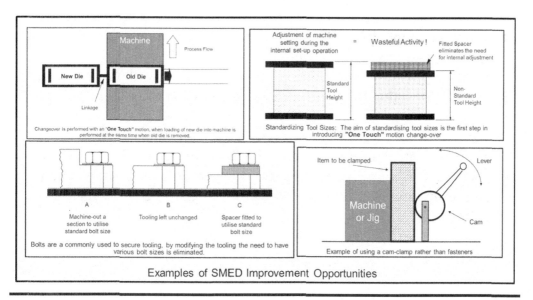

Figure 3.19   SMED improvement techniques.

Standardized Work (a.k.a. Standard Work)

Standard Work is the detailed definition of the most efficient method (activities, tasks, etc.) to produce a product (or perform a service) at a balanced rate to achieve a desired output rate (takt time). It breaks down the work into job elements, which will be sequenced, organized, and, hopefully, repeatedly followed by associates.

The purpose of Standard Work is:

■ to determine the best combination of worker and equipment tasks grouped together such that the sum of the individual task times is less than or equal to takt time (customer requirements);
■ to establish the best-known method for performing a task (the associates work together to establish the best way);
■ to achieve balance between all tasks in a process;
■ to establish and clarify the guidelines for production (quality, cost, staffing, inventory, and safety);
■ to provide a baseline for continuous improvement.

For Standard Work to be effective; each step in the process must be well defined and executed repeatedly in the same manner, because any variations in the execution will typically increase cycle time and cause quality issues. Standard Work describes how a process should consistently be executed and documents current "best practices." It provides a baseline from which a better approach can be developed, allowing continuous improvement methods to leverage learning.

Establishing precise procedures for each operator's work (i.e. Standard Work) in a production or service process is based on three elements:

1. Takt time, which is the rate at which products must be made in a process to meet customer demand – formally defined, takt time is the rate at which your customer buys a product. It is often called the drum-beat of production, since once takt time is calculated all

processes should rhythmically operate at, or preferably a bit below, takt time.

2. The precise work sequence in which an operator performs tasks within takt time. It is extremely important to determine the best and most efficient way for operators to perform their work. It helps ensure your process maintains consistency and stability. Whenever possible, our aim should be to limit wasted motion, reaching, or any other non-value-added movement.

3. The standard inventory, including units in machines, required to keep the process operating smoothly. Standard inventory is actually referred to as Standard Work-in-Process (SWIP). SWIP is the minimum necessary in-process inventory (work-in-process or WIP) to maintain Standard Work.

Standardized work, once established and displayed at workstations, is the object of continuous improvement through kaizens. The benefits of standardized work include documentation of the current process for all shifts, reductions in variability, easier training of new operators, reductions in injuries and strain, and a baseline for improvement activities.

The components of Standard Work can be seen in Figure 3.20.

Components	Purpose
Routing-by-Walking Around (RBWA)	Process Overview
Time Observation Sheet	Motion & Time Study
Standard Work Combination Sheet	Man-Machine Relationship
Process Capacity Sheet	Capacity Analysis
Yamazumi Chart	Productivity Analysis
Routing-by-Walking Around (RBWA)	Value-Added Analysis
Standard Work Sheet (SWS)	Cell or Line Set-Up
Job Element Breakdown Sheet (JEBS)	Job Instructions
Visual Aids	Supplement JEBS

Figure 3.20   Standard work's components and purposes.

Routing-By-Walking-Around___Analysis Form

Product Line:
Part Number: Page ___ of __
Part Name: Prepared By:
Date:

Operation		Time (seconds)		Distance Traveled (feet)	Analysis of Time								Notes
Step	Description	Cumulative	Each		V	I	E	W	T	M	S	N	

Basic Instructions:
1) Staple yourself to an order or part
2) List the tasks (steps) you go through... in order; do not skip any
3) Take time data for each step
4) Classify with "Analysis of Time"
5) Determine improvement opportunities

V = Value-Adding Step
I = Internal Inspection (Own Work)
E = External Inspect
W = Wait / Queue
T = Material Transport
M = Motion
S = Storage / Inventory
N = Non-Value-Added but Required

Figure 3.21 Routing by Walking Around (RBWA) template.

Routing By Walking Around (RBWA) (Figure 3.21)

The RBWA was explained in detail in the assessment tool and methodology section earlier.

> As a Standard Work element, the RBWA provides a high-level overview of the entire process, so it's a planning tool as you embark on a Standard Work initiative.

As you proceed farther along your Standard Work implementation program, the RBWA is an analysis tool to help you identify improvement opportunities, i.e. eliminating the seven wastes (TIMWOOD) and non-value-added activities.

Time Observation Sheet (Figure 3.22)

The Time Observation Sheet is used to record cycle times during the development of Standard Work. It's a sheet for conducting a time study of an operation, process, etc.

The Time Observation Sheet is used to record the elements of work/activity that the operator is performing and to generate a reasonable amount of time required to perform these work elements. The Time Observation Sheet is used to establish initial cycle times for all operators and their activities being performed. A work element is defined as the smallest increment of work that could be moved from one person to another.

Time Observation Sheet	Proccess: Observer / Timer:													Date:		
			Timed Data										Lowest Repeatable Time	Lowest Repeatable Time + Allowance	Remarks
#	Work Element		1	2	3	4	5	6	7	8	9	10			
		Clock Running Time														
		Elapsed Time														
		Clock Running Time														
		Elapsed Time														
		Clock Running Time														
		Elapsed Time														
		Clock Running Time														
		Elapsed Time														
		Clock Running Time														
		Elapsed Time														
		Clock Running Time														
		Elapsed Time														
		Clock Running Time														
		Elapsed Time														
		Clock Running Time														
		Elapsed Time														
		Clock Running Time														
		Elapsed Time														
		Clock Running Time														
		Elapsed Time														
		Clock Running Time														
		Elapsed Time														
		Clock Running Time														
		Elapsed Time														
		Clock Running Time														
		Elapsed Time														
		Clock Running Time														
		Elapsed Time														
		Clock Running Time														
		Elapsed Time														
		Clock Running Time														
		Elapsed Time														
		Total Time for 1 Cycle														Total of Lowest Repeatable Elements

Figure 3.22   Time Observation Sheet template.

The steps to filling out a Time Observation Sheet are:

■ observe the steps that the operator goes through to complete one cycle of work;
■ record those observed steps on the Time Observation Sheet; ask the operator to perform the same series of steps for the next ten cycles as closely as possible;
■ time and record the running time for each element for ten cycles (videotaping is optional);
■ calculate and record the cycle time for each cycle of work;
■ the lowest repeated times becomes the new current standards. If none are repeatable, then choose the second lowest times;
■ apply a personal allowance factor of 12% to account for fatigue, breaks, etc. The allowance is a subjective factor but typically resides between 8 and ~15%, although some choose to omit. I have found 12% to be a nice choice for assembly operations.

Standard Work Combination Sheet (Figure 3.23)

The Standard Work Combination Sheet (SWCS) shows the combination of manual work time, walk time, and machine processing time for each operation in a production sequence. It can be very helpful to identify the waste of waiting and overburden and to confirm Standard WIP (SWIP or Standard Work-in-Process).

Key points in regard to the SWCS include:

- shows the combination of manual and machine work for one operator; identifies how much work each operator can perform within the takt time (i.e. a tool to help balance the operators);
- graphically displays the different types of time; i.e. manual, automatic, walking, waiting, and takt time;
- allows the re-combining of work to accommodate changes in demand, processes, and/or available time;
- Dedicate one form for each operator (don't combine operators on the same form).

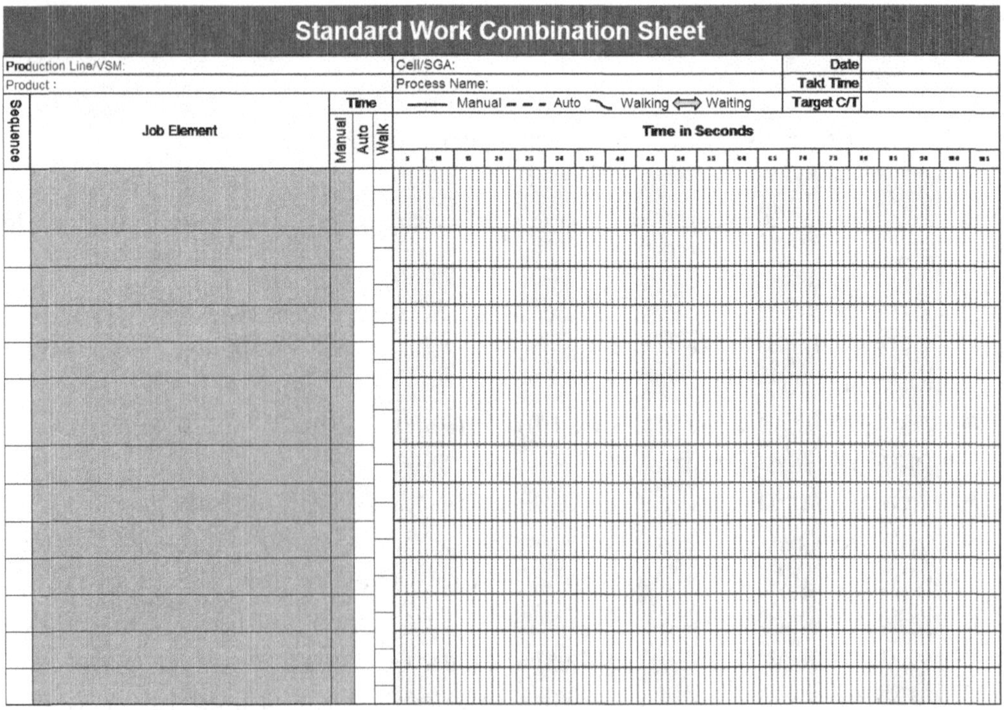

Figure 3.23 Standard Work Combination Sheet template.

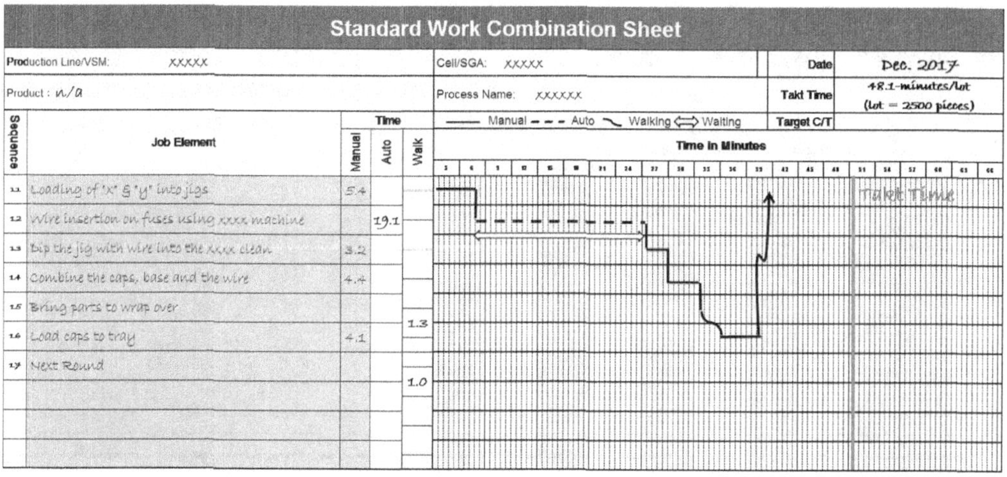

Figure 3.24   Example: Completed Standard Work Combination Sheet.

The simple steps to complete a SWCS are:

■ Fill in the sequence numbers indicating the sequence in which the operator carries out operations. The sequence numbers are extracted from the Time Observation Sheet.
■ Operation: Enter in the element description from the Time Observation Sheet.
■ Add the appropriate times to the SWCS.
  – *Walk time*: Enter the time it takes to move to the next station. Do not distinguish between whether the operator is carrying anything or not.
  – *Manual time*: Enter the time for human tasks from Time Observation Sheet.
  – *Machine time (auto)*: Enter the time for the automatic cycle for the machine task from the RBWA (a.k.a. Routing By Walking Around).
  – Graph the work content utilizing the legend (manual, auto, walking, or waiting) (Figures 3.23 and 3.24).

Process Capacity Chart (Figure 3.25)

The purpose of the Process Capacity Chart is to determine a given process's capacity for a shift and thus its ability to meet takt time. This determination is made by calculating each process step's capacity, which considers the available time per shift, completion time, tool-change time, and other factors as required for each single workpiece (or lot, jig, etc.).

Process Capacity Table											
Part / Product			Cell / Process			Takt Time or Customer Demand				Date	
						Demand per Shift				Prepared By	
Step	Work Process Description	Machine Number or Name	Basic Time			Tool Changeover Time			Summary		Remarks
			Manual Time (A)	Auto Time (B)	Total (C = A+B)	Changeover Time (D)	Units per Change (E)	Time / Unit (F = D/E)	Total Time per Unit (G = C+F)	Process Capacity (H = Shift / G)	
1					0						
2					0						
3					0						
4					0						
5					0						
6					0						
7					0						
8					0						
9					0						
10					0						
11					0						
12					0						
13					0						
14					0						
15					0						

Figure 3.25 Process Capacity Chart template.

The process's overall capacity is defined by its bottleneck, which may be minimized through improvement activities like changeover time reduction (or SMED) and machine/operator cycle-time reduction (eliminate waste) (Figure 3.25).

Yamazumi Chart

A Yamazumi Chart may be a new component of Standard Work or maybe totally new terminology for you. So, Yamazumi Charts: What are they?

Yamazumi is a Japanese word that literally means to stack up.

A Yamazumi Chart (or Yamazumi Board) is a stacked bar chart that shows the source of the cycle time for a process. The chart is used to graphically represent processes for optimization purposes.

Process tasks are individually represented in a stacked bar chart; these can be categorized as value added, non-value added, or waste. The mean duration time of each task is recorded and displayed within the bar chart. Each process task is stacked to represent the entire process step.

The Yamazumi Chart's y-axis (vertical) represents cycle time. Its x-axis (horizontal) represents an individual operator (or workstation).

A target cycle time will often be plotted to aid line balancing activities. Adding the targeted takt time is not optional.

The Yamazumi Chart can be used for both process waste elimination or line balancing activity. Process steps can be rearranged or deleted to optimize and balance the target process.

The Yamazumi Chart is intended to support Lean Transformation activities or any continuous improvement teams.

In summary, a Yamazumi Chart is a visual tool to help:

■ balance work between operators and workstations;
■ identify and prioritize opportunities for improvement (i.e. minimize non-value-added tasks / elements);
■ track improvement efforts (create a Yamazumi Board in the work area) (Figures 3.26a,b and 3.27).

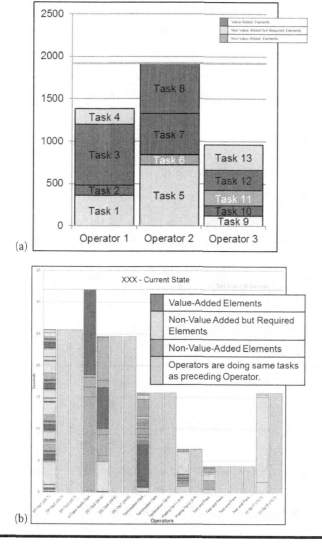

Figure 3.26   (a) Basic Yamazumi Chart (b) Current State Yamazumi Chart.

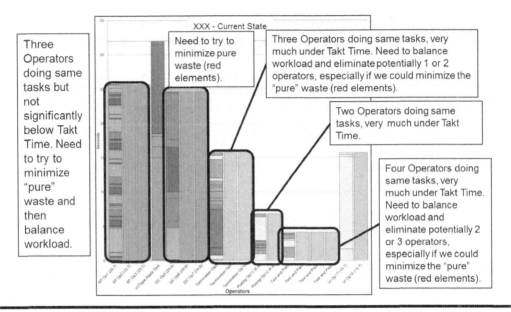

Figure 3.27   What does the Yamazumi Chart tell you?

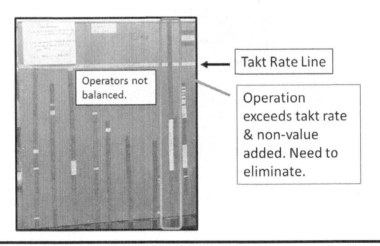

Figure 3.28   Working Yamazumi Board.

Excel can be utilized to create a Yamazumi Chart, or there are many sources of formularized Yamazumi-specific Excel-based templates available online. Or you may choose to create one manually, i.e. a Yamazumi Board.

A Yamazumi Board is a visual representation of the operators and their work elements and is typically displayed within the work area. It's a Yamazumi Chart, but it's more of a working / living medium to allow continuous improvement by operators, technicians, engineers, etc.

The Yamazumi Board provides a mechanism to quickly rebalance a process when takt time changes and creates a visual indication of operations that are overloaded (beyond takt time) or which may be underutilized (Figure 3.28).

Standard Work Sheet

A Standard Work Sheet (SWS) consists of all elements for a specific operation (cell, line, etc.), including each step involved in the process and the approximate amount of time required for that process.

Elements included within SWS are inspection points, safety concerns, process bottleneck, Standard WIP, process lead time, process flow, and number of operators, all relative to the required takt time.

With a Standard Work Sheet, you are able:

■ to document the best combination of manpower, material, and machines;
■ show the work sequence (process flow) for all operators in a cell;
■ identify safety, quality, and Standard WIP points (Figures 3.29 and 3.30).

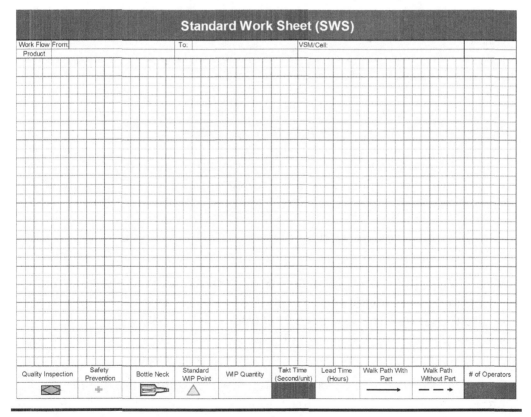

Figure 3.29   Standard Work Sheet (SWS) template.

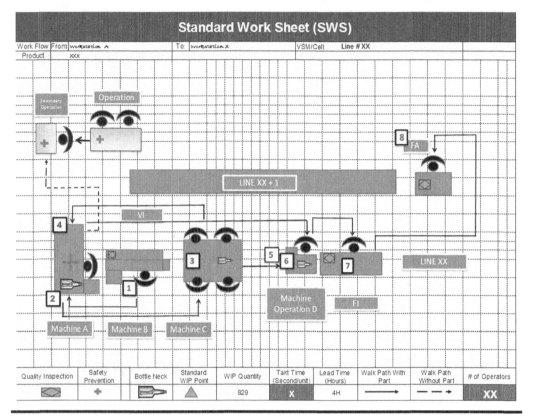

Figure 3.30   Example: Standard Work Sheet (SWS).

Job Element Breakdown Sheet (JEBS) (Figure 3.31)

The Job Element Breakdown Sheet (JEBS) is also often referred to as Standard Work instructions as the JEBS focuses on the work of a single operator.

The JEBS provides an operator with:

- sequential description of work tasks denoting key operational, quality, and safety considerations / points;
- visual references for operational clarity;
- a quick visual reference / reminder.

The JEBS is the key component of the TWI (Training Within Industry) approach and should be the primary job-specific document for training new operators (Figure 3.31).

Job Element Breakdown Sheet				
Description of the task:				List Common Key Points:
Parts (UPN, describe the parts)				
Tools & supplies required:				
Safety equipment required:				
Important Steps		**Key Points**	**Reasons**	Training Aid: (put hand sketches, diagrams, parts, or layouts here. Insert digital pictures if available.)
WHAT?	A logical segment of the operation	HOW? Things in important steps that will: 1. make or break the job 2. injure the worker 3. make the work easier	WHY? Why the key points is key?	
1				
2				
3				
4				
5				
6				
7				
8				
9				
10				
11				
12				
Key Point reminders:	□ Critical check or inspection	△ Quantity check ✚ Could injure the person	✓ Makes the job easier	Owner of This Document: / Page of / Rev #: / Date:

Figure 3.31 Job Element Breakdown Sheet (JEBS) template.

The steps for completing a JEBS are:

■ Complete the information on the JEBS form about the job, i.e. description of task (job), part info, tools, safety equipment, etc.
■ Complete the "What?" – a logical sequence of the operation:
  – List major steps in sequence (taken from the Process Observation Form or Time Observation Sheet).
  – Start the "step" description with a verb.
■ Complete the "How?" – things that are important within a step, that will:
  – make or break the job; i.e. critical elements;
  – possibly cause injury to the worker;
  – make the work easier to perform ("tricks of the trade" based on experience).
■ Complete the "Why?" – the key points are key because they are
  – critical to quality or customer satisfaction (internal or external customers);
  – critical to the form, fit, or function of a part;
  – critical safety or equipment factor.

■ Complete the "Visual Aids" section of the JEBS form.
  – You can insert a picture, sketch, process flow into the visual aid area that will serve as quick reference for the operator as they perform the tasks.
  – These visual aids should also be a training aid when training new operators.

NOTE: You don't necessarily have to have a "How" or "Why" for every step, only for those steps that have a significant "How" or "Why" within them. The same applies to the visual aids (add only if they add value); see Visual Aids section below (Figure 3.32).In summary, JEBS should:

Job Element Breakdown Sheet							
Description of the task:		Draw a Turtle					**List Common Key Points:**
Parts (UPN, describe the parts)							Turtle should be centered horizontally & vertically on paper.
Tools & supplies required:		1 sheet blank paper & pencil					
Safety equipment required:		None					
Important Steps		**Key Points**			**Reasons**		**Training Aid:** (put hand sketches, diagrams, parts, or layouts here. Insert digital pictures if available.)
WHAT?	A logical segment of the operation	**HOW?**	Things in important steps that will: 1. make or break the job 2. injure the worker 3. make the work easier		**WHY?**	Why the key points is key?	
1	Take a blank sheet of paper and divide (draw) none equal boxes	9 boxes should be of equal size and spread proportionally vertically & horizontally (3 x 3).		✓	This is the "standardized" grid for drawing our Turtle.		
2	Draw an Oval	Oval should extend to all 9 boxes with the majority being in the center box.			Oval must be centered in page. This is the Turtle's body (shell).		
3	Draw an Small Oval centered with large oval	Oval should be in Top-Middle box and 3/4 of should extend past top of large oval.			This is the Turtle's head.		
4	Draw two small ovals.	3/4 of oval should extend past large oval in the top-left & top-right squares respectively.			Center of oval should be about 45° from large oval. This Turtle's front legs.		
5	Draw two small ovals.	3/4 of oval should extend past large oval in the bottom-left & bottom-right squares respectively.			Center of oval should be about 45° from large oval. This Turtle's back legs.		
6	Draw two small black circles. Draw small, narrow triangle.	Two black circles in top-small oval (horizontally upper-center). Draw small triangle extending from bottom-center of large oval.			These are the Turtle's eyes & tail.		
7	Draw hexagon .	Draw hexagon perfectly center horizontally & vertically in large oval. Draw straight line connecting upper & lower points of hexagon with upper & lower center points of oval.			This is part of the Turtle's shell design.		
8	Draw diagonal line across large oval.	Connect diagonal a left upper oval's (leg) lower intersection with large oval & hexagon's upper left corner. Repeat for lower-right oval's upper intersection and lower right corner of hexagon.			This is part of the Turtle's shell design.		
9	Draw diagonal line across large oval.	Connect diagonal a right upper oval's (leg) lower intersection with large oval & hexagon's upper right corner. Repeat for lower-left oval's upper intersection and lower left corner of hexagon.			This is part of the Turtle's shell design.		
Key Point reminders:	☐ **Critical check or inspection**	△ **Quantity check**	✚ **Could injure the person**		✓ **Makes the job easier**	**Owner of This Document:**	**Page** of **Rev #:** **Date:**

Figure 3.32 Example: Job Element Breakdown Sheet (JEBS).

■ be simple, common sense reminders to the operator on what's critical about the job that they're performing;

■ be simple, common sense reminders to the trainer of what needs to be covered in training a new operator;

■ be thorough, but it's equally important that they're simple and concise.

Visual Aids (Figure 3.33)

The Visual Aid Sheet is a type of job instruction that should be displayed at the operator's workstation; it is most often utilized to supplement the JEBS, as the JEBS has limited space for visual aids.

The Visual Aid Sheet should be used to highlight key points in safety, quality, or customer requirements (Figure 3.33).

In summary, Standard Work defines the way that a task should be performed.

VISUAL AID								

ORIGINATOR	APPROVED BY	TITLE	DOC NO	REV.	REF. DOC	STATION / PROCESS	DATE	PAGE NO
								_ OF _

Figure 3.33   Visual Aid template.

Standard Work …

■ is a major tool to reduce variations in the way everyone executes their roles along the value streams and should be deployed across all functions, including the leadership team;

■ is a countermeasure for process irregularities; the most common form of standardization is Standard (or Standardized) Work. The powerfulness of Standard Work doesn't really resonate from the Standard Work documents but from the activities that develop the Standard Work (RBWA, time observations, man–machine relationships, process capacity, and the Yamazumi);

■ has a creation standard that requires the thorough understanding of the work activities and the work elements that comprise the activities. The creation of Standard Work is a collaborative effort to define the best way to perform a task or activity and, like most elements of Lean, is a combination of "science" and "art" along with a certain amount of common sense.

The basis of most Standard Work is the time studying of the work activities or tasks and the breaking down of the activities into work elements. Work elements are defined as the smallest increment of work that could be moved from one person to another; this is important to optimize the balancing of work between operators. One the best tools for optimizing the balancing of work between operators is the Yamazumi Chart (also known as an Operator Balancing Sheet). But the distinguishing difference between a Yamazumi Chart and an Operator Balancing Sheet is the differentiation between value-added work elements and non-value-added elements.

The flow diagram in Figure 3.34 shows a typical sequence for creating Standard Work.

Another key form of Standard Work is Leader Standard Work.

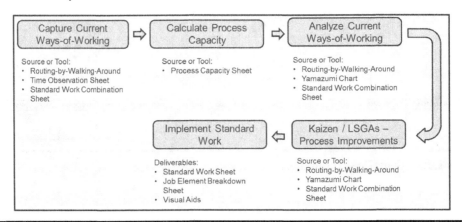

Figure 3.34 Typical sequence for creating and implementing Standard Work.

Leader Standard Work (Figure 3.35)

Leader Standard Work changes the role of leaders (managers, supervisors, engineers, cell leaders, etc.) from primarily being the problem solvers (i.e. firefighters) to building the overall capabilities of their subordinates to collaboratively and systematically solve problems and continuously improve all processes.

The key elements of Leader Standard Work are:

■ Gemba Walks;
■ tiered meetings;
■ coaching and mentoring subordinates;
■ continuously improving safety, quality, delivery, and cost; and
■ improving oneself.

Case-in-Point Example 3.12 Standardized Work

Actually, my first involvement in Standardized Work goes back to the late-seventies. I had just been promoted to Engineering Manager in a fast-growing telecommunication manufacturing environment. We were implementing new printed circuit board assemblies (PCBAs) into production at seemingly sub-sonic speeds, and the training curve for our completely (100%) recently hired production staff had to be immediate. This definitely preceded Lean

Figure 3.35   Leader Standard Work example.

manufacturing and even just-in-time manufacturing, so I had to fend for myself. Production at the time was using engineering drawings (bill of materials, assembly drawings, schematics, etc.) to assemble thousands of PCBAs. It was obvious that "engineering drawings" couldn't be used in a fast-paced, high-volume, high-mix production environment, So, I had to come up with a solution quickly. The solution was to create Shop Aids; not sure where (or how) that terminology came about, but my team and I knew what a Shop Aid had to deliver – i.e. a combination of visual aids with key pertinent assembly instructions. It had to be very simple but also very detailed and concise.

We designed a simple two-page format. The top page was an illustration of the component with the PCB and its insertion location identified. The lower page had the part number, quantity, engineering code, and any special instructions. All of these pages had to be created manually and hand-drawn; these were the days before the proliferation of computer-generated graphics. And all of the instructions, etc. were hand-written. I was hiring temporary workers who were unemployed or retired artists. Our Shop Aids were artistically beautiful, but most importantly, they were very effective.

We could change products quickly, as each workstation had multiple sets of Shop Aids within arm's-reach.

We divided the PCBs into quadrants, and a single operator would do a single quadrant. The boards were fairly symmetrical in their layout, so the operators were fairly balanced by default.

A prerequisite to the Shop Aids was a detailed process router (a work sequence) for each PCBA. The router and the bill of material would be key elements for the Shop Aid creation; the engineering assembly drawing may be used if the PCBA included heatsinks, large transformers, and/or any mechanical devices (most of our PCBAs had a metal faceplate and ejector-levers).

Bottom line, this company never could had grown to the number one digital telecommunication manufacturer in the world (in the 1980s) without the development and implementation of these manually created Shop Aids. A couple years after this initial Shop Aid deployment, our computer capabilities grew and we were able to convert over to computer-enabled documents, but we didn't deviate from the original design and content.

Visual Management

Visual Management entails managing the business via visual controls and, maybe most importantly, being able to identify any abnormalities at a moment's glance (< 30 seconds).

Visual Management is achieved by organizing, in plain view, all tools, materials, production activities, and production system performance indicators so that the status of the system can be understood at a glance by everyone involved. This is often referred to the "30-second rule" – i.e. anyone should be able to come into an area and, within 30 seconds, be able to determine the operational and performance status of the area. (Note: There are variances on the 30-second rule such as the 10-second or 20-second rule.)

Remember the old … the very old saying, a picture is worth a thousand words? Well, that's what Visual Management is about. It's about putting the visual mechanisms in place that allow anyone entering the area to quickly differentiate between conforming and non-conforming activities and, particularly, to be able to quickly identify any abnormalities within the processes, flow, workplace, workforce, etc.

A key element of any Visual Management mechanism is the incorporation of the colors green and red. ALWAYS use green to mean or represent that we are meeting or exceeding a target, objective, or goal; use red to signify that we are not meeting the required expectations. So, if you look at any communication board, etc., you will immediately be able to hone in on anything that is red to identify that there's an issue. Some folks will use yellow to signify marginally failing, but the fact is that you've either met/exceeded or failed; there is no in-between.

Some common types of Visual Management mechanisms include:

■ *Hour-by-hour board*: This is one of my favorite visual controls. An hour-by-hour board (HBHB) monitors actual production output versus targeted production output on an hour-by-hour basis. The output target most often reflects the takt rate as it's determined by actual customer demand. But regardless of how it's determined, the HBHB will reflect the desired output of a department, manufacturing, or business cell/ line, etc. (usually stated in black), and then the actual output is written on the board in either green or red: i.e. we're either making the target or missing it. The reason that we want to make the timeframe an hour is to reflect urgency in addressing any issues that may arise, e.g. material shortages, equipment/facilities downtime, worker productivity, absenteeism, etc. (Figures 3.36a,b).

  The HBHB should be sized about 2 × 4 feet (A3 or 10.5" × 14" minimum) and prominently displayed at the front of each department, cell, line, etc. There can be significant flexibility in the size and location of the HBHBs, but as you decide how to proceed, think about compliance with the 30-second rule.

Production Board (Hour-by-Hour Production)

	Date:		Week Day:		Dept. / Cell:		Shift:		

Hour Marker	Hourly Time Marker	Plan	Actual	Variance	Reason for Variance	Supervisor Sign Off	Manager Sign Off	Site Leader Sign Off
1								
2								
3								
4								
5								
6								
7								
8								
9								
10								
11								
12								

(a)   Hour-by-Hour Generic Template

Production Board (Hour-by-Hour Production)

Date: 12/25/2019   Week Day: Monday   Dept. / Cell: XY Assembly #1   Shift: Day

Hour Marker	Hourly Time Marker	Plan	Actual	Variance	Reason for Variance	Supervisor Sign Off	Manager Sign Off	Site Leader Sign Off
1	6:00 – 7:00	200 / 200	202 / 202	+2 / +2	2 units lefover from night-shift	Ray		
2	7:00 – 8:00	400 / 200	400 / 198	0 / -2	short team meeting	Ray		
3	8:00 – 9:00	600 / 200	600 / 200	0 / 0		Ray		
4	9:00 – 10:00	800 / 200	800 / 200	0 / 0		Ray	RK	
5	10:00 – 11:00	1000 / 200	1000 / 200	0 / 0		Ray		JMK
6	11:00 – 12:00	1200 / 200	1164 / 164	-36 / -36	Press machine down. Electrical short.	Ray		
7	12:00 – 13:00	1400 / 200	1374 / 210	-26 / +10		Ray		
8	13:00 – 14:00	1600 / 200	1586 / 212	-14 / +12		Ray		
9	14:00 – 15:00	1800 / 200	1786 / 200	-14 / 0		Fred	RK	
10	15:00 – 16:00	2000 / 200	2000 / 214	0 / +14		Fred		
11	16:00 – 17:00	2200 / 200	2197 / 197	-3 / -3	inserter machine jammed. Operator fixed.	Fred		
12	17:00 – 18:00	2400 / 200	2398 / 201	-2 / +1		Fred		

(b)   Hour-by-Hour Board Example

Production Board (Hour-by-Hour Production)

Date: 12/25/2019   Week Day: Monday   Dept. / Cell: XY Assembly #1   Shift: Day

Hour Marker	Hourly Time Marker	Plan	Actual	Variance	A1	A2	A3	P1	P2	I	T	FI	Reason for Variance	Supervisor Sign Off	Manager Sign Off	Site Leader Sign Off
					Workstations w/ Variance											
1	6:00 – 7:00	200 / 200	202 / 202	+2 / +2									2 units lefover from night-shift	Ray		
2	7:00 – 8:00	400 / 200	400 / 198	0 / -2									short team meeting	Ray		
3	8:00 – 9:00	600 / 200	600 / 200	0 / 0										Ray		
4	9:00 – 10:00	800 / 200	800 / 200	0 / 0										Ray	RK	
5	10:00 – 11:00	1000 / 200	1000 / 200	0 / 0										Ray		JMK
6	11:00 – 12:00	1200 / 200	1164 / 164	-36 / -36					▮				Press machine down. Electrical short.	Ray		
7	12:00 – 13:00	1400 / 200	1374 / 210	-26 / +10										Ray		
8	13:00 – 14:00	1600 / 200	1586 / 212	-14 / +12										Ray		
9	14:00 – 15:00	1800 / 200	1786 / 200	-14 / 0										Fred	RK	
10	15:00 – 16:00	2000 / 200	2000 / 214	0 / +14										Fred		
11	16:00 – 17:00	2200 / 200	2197 / 197	-3 / -3						▮			inserter machine jammed. Operator fixed.	Fred		
12	17:00 – 18:00	2400 / 200	2398 / 201	-2 / +1										Fred		

(c)   Hour-by-Hour Board - Workstation Breakdown Example

Figure 3.36   **(a, b) Examples of an hour-by-hour board (blank and filled-in). (c) Example of an hour-by-hour board with workstation monitoring.**

The signatures of the appropriate parties state that they have visited the area (the Gemba) and have taken the appropriate action in regard to the area's performance. This activity should be part of the individual's Leader Standard Work.

■ *Key visual mechanisms evolved from 5S*. 5S is the Lean terminology for workplace organization. And 5S's mantra (paraphrased) is "everything has a place and everything is in its place". There are several mechanisms within 5S to support the 30-second rule:
  - *Shadow boards*: Shadow boards show the location where a tool should be stored; an empty spot means a tool etc. is being used or maybe wasn't put away properly.
  - *Floor marking*: This can be used to control the amount of inventory (kanbans, bins, pallets, etc.) that should be in an area (both maximum and a minimum); an empty spot or an overflowing area may signify a process abnormality.
  - *Red floor marking or red bins*: These should signify non-conforming material or product (scrap, rejects, damaged, customer returns, etc.).
  - *Red tag Area*: This is an area where unused items are stored for dispositioning.

  All of the above make good audit points for a Leader's Gemba Walk.

■ *Communication boards*: These proliferate in "Lean" companies and have varying degrees of effectiveness. I've already stated my fondness for hour-by-hour boards. In a Lean / continuous improvement environment, it's very common for every department, manufacturing area, work team, etc. to have a board to communicate its activities. Most boards of this type would include:
  - relevant safety (respect for people), quality, delivery, and productivity (or cost) metrics;
  - improvement initiatives, etc.

  It's often stated that communication boards should adhere to a 10-second rule; i.e. that it should take no more than 10-seconds to look at an area's or team's communication board to determine its "health". Incorporating green and red notations (met/exceeded or missed, respectively) should easily accommodate a 10-second rule.

- *Value Stream Map (VSM)*: These displays or boards are a very common Lean Visual Management tool. An effective VSM board should be a fluid tool. VSM boards should at a minimum reflect the current state of the value stream and should be populated with "kaizen bursts" denoting improvement opportunities. There should be a scorecard showing key metrics (e.g. process lead time, value-added ratios, etc.) for the current, future, and ideal states. There should also be some type of project status summary and/or timeline for prioritized improvement initiatives.

Case-in-Point Example 3.13 Visual Management (an American Manufacturer in SE Asia)

I'll share with you a simple Visual Management implementation case story. The background is that this company would email their performance (daily output) at the end of each shift, and the manufacturing team would meet the following morning to discuss what went wrong, recovery plans, etc. Additionally, there were large TV monitors exhibiting the overall daily performance rate versus takt rate (requirement of units per hour and accumulated throughout the day).

The issue of the TV monitors was that you might be able to tell if you were missing or meeting the overall output requirements, but you didn't know where any downfalls occurred, i.e. it didn't give you a clear picture of where issues resided.

Although the shift-ending emails were informative, they were too late to respond to any shortfalls in a timely manner.

The solution was that we simply implemented hour-by-hour boards at strategic upstream and downstream locations, and the hour-by-hour-boards were updated hourly (duh!). The cell leaders would undertake immediate countermeasures against any shortfalls, and there was a documented escalation plan to address unresolved issues.

Total Productive Maintenance (TPM)

Total Productive Maintenance (TPM) is a set of techniques, originally pioneered by the Toyota Group (Japan), to ensure that every machine in a production process is consistently able to perform its required tasks.

TPM consists of three major underlying principles:

1. total participation of all associates, e.g. maintenance personnel, engineers (manufacturing, equipment, etc.), quality experts, operators, and management;

2. achieving total productivity of equipment by focusing on the six major losses of equipment productivity, i.e. downtime, changeovers, minor stoppages, equipment speed losses, product scrap, and product rework;
3. total-life cycle management of equipment (cradle to grave) to revise maintenance practices, activities, and improvements relative to its stage of its life cycle.

There are eight widely accepted pillars of TPM that are mostly focused on proactive and preventative techniques for improving equipment effectiveness. It places responsibility for routine maintenance, such as cleaning, lubricating, and inspection, in the hands of operators (i.e. autonomous maintenance).

TPM's eight pillars are:

1. Autonomous Maintenance
- place responsibility for routine maintenance, such as cleaning, lubricating, and inspection, in the hands of operators.

2. Focused Improvement
- have small groups of employees work together proactively to achieve regular, incremental improvements in equipment operation, e.g. OEE-driven, SGA (Small Group Activities), kaizens, etc.;
- use OEE (overall equipment effectiveness) as a key baseline metric to gauge improvement effectiveness;
- use SMED (Single-Minute Exchange of Dies) as a key component of any improvement initiative.

3. Planned Maintenance
- schedule maintenance tasks based on predicted and/or measured failure rates.

4. Quality Management
- design error detection and prevention into production processes; utilize a Machine Failure Mode and Effect Analysis (MFMEA);
- apply A3 problem solving and Root Cause Analysis to eliminate recurring sources of quality defects.

5. Early/Equipment Management
- direct practical knowledge and understanding of manufacturing equipment gained through TPM toward improving the design of new equipment;

   – utilize a Machine Failure Mode and Effect Analysis (MFMEA) to proactively address potential new equipment issues.
6. **Education and Training**
   – fill in knowledge gaps necessary to achieve TPM goals; applies to
   operators, maintenance personnel, and managers;
   – implement a technician scorecard for cross-training and full skillset
   and knowledge coverage.
7. **Safety Health Environment**
   – maintain a safe and healthy working environment;
   – deployment of 5S principles;
   – eliminate muri (overburdening of man and machine); ensure
   principle of motions are followed and ergonomic best practices
   adhered to.
8. **Administrative and Office TPM**
   – apply TPM techniques to administrative functions:
     • autonomous maintenance of office equipment;
     • 6S deployment;
     • focused improvement from SGA (Small Group Activities).

Overall Equipment Effectiveness (OEE)

OEE is a metric that identifies the percentage of planned production time that
is truly productive. It is a measure of the effectiveness of a TPM program.

OEE is calculated as the product of performance (P), availability (A), and
quality (Q) – P × A × Q, where:

■ Performance (P) represents the theoretical ideal performance of the measured equipment. So, the "baseline" performance that an equipment is
   being measured against should be the performance that can be obtained
   if the equipment produces the maximum output (total units) that can be
   obtained when the equipment is operated at maximum speed (designed
   speed). It's the unbiased "ideal" performance of the equipment. Besides
   not being able to run a machine at its optimal speed, the other area that
   significantly affects performance is ad-hoc minor stoppages.
■ Availability (A) is best defined as the percentage of time that equipment
   is available to produce parts (i.e. "saleable" parts). Availability's baseline
   should be 24 hours, 7 days/week. The only acceptable deductions from this
   baseline should be for hours that no production is planned or scheduled

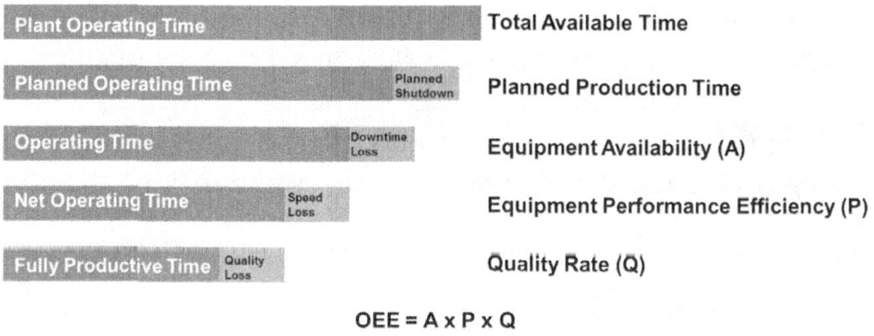

Figure 3.37   The components of OEE.

(e.g. facility shutdowns, non-working hours, scheduled breaks/meals, etc.), or hours when there's no actual demand. Any other equipment stoppage should be viewed as an opportunity for improvement. Stoppages will be required for maintenance, changeovers, engineering-time, etc., but they should be viewed as opportunities for uptime improvements, i.e. faster changeovers, autonomous maintenance, shorter downtime due to maintenance or repairs, efficient engineering runs (or after-hours), etc.

■ Quality (Q) is the percentage of goods parts produced (i.e. parts that meet all specifications). This element is one of the weaknesses of OEE, as real-time quality data is not always readily available so often the Q component of the equation defaults to 100%, which defeats the purpose/benefit of measuring OEE (Figure 3.37).

An example of an OEE calculation is:

■ *Performance*: If the ideal (or designed) output of machine is 2,000 units/day, and the actual total units produced that day was 1,800, then the performance would be 1,800 ÷ 2,000 = 90.0%.
■ *Availability*: If the "production" day is scheduled to be 21 hours/day (3 hours unscheduled, i.e. breaks/meals), but the equipment actually only ran for 19.5 hours due to changeovers and minor ad-hoc stoppages, then the availability would be calculated as 19.5 ÷ 21 = 92.9%.
■ *Quality*: If a total of 1,800 units were produced but only 1,770 units were good, then quality would be 1,770 ÷ 1,800 = 98.3%.

The OEE (P × A × Q) for this scenario would be calculated as 90.0% × 92.9% × 98.3% = 82.2% (therefore, probably a best-in-class type performance).

If an organization diligently follows the criteria above for calculating OEE, then consistently reaching an OEE of > 80% may be very difficult. But, in my opinion, OEE is not meant to be a performance / benchmarking metric; measuring OEE gives you a continuous improvement metric to assist in improving overall utilization of your resources and making them more effective.

OEE allows an organization to:

- analyze the gap between ideal / design performance versus actual;
- ensure Standardized Work is effectively deployed and non-standardized activities are eliminated;
- reduce lost time for required activities such as preventative maintenance, changeovers, engineering trials, completing repairs, etc. and differentiate and analyze special and common causes;
- increase repair / reliability metrics, mean time between failures / fix / repair (MTBF / MTBR), mean time to repair / failure (MTTR / MTTF), or failure in time (FIT);
- conduct Root Cause Analysis of gaps in current equipment performance versus ideal equipment performance.

> *Let me go off on a brief tangent with a bit of a sidebar on OEE: I have been involved in many discussions on OEE (overall equipment effectiveness) over my career, and I've seen OEE evolve over the past 10 years or so ... in a negative way. When I first learned of OEE as a Key Performance Indicator (KPI) over 20 years ago, I didn't really get the "love" for it. Over the past 20 years, I've definitely seen it misused more than I've seen it being deployed effectively. And 20 years ago, a world-class OEE for discrete manufacturers was 60~70%; today, world class is touted as 85~90%. Have companies improved that much? My opinion is No! But companies have become more liberal in their application of OEE.*
>
> *OEE can be a very effective metric if utilized as an analytic metric to drive improvement, but to be effective, OEE should be reflective of the actual true output of customer-shippable good devices versus the ideal theoretical output of the equipment (or cell or whatever you're measuring). I've seen companies removing engineering-time from the "availability" component OEE calculation, but the fact is that if you spent one hour for engineering (or whatever), that's one hour that you're not making product that's saleable to the customer. It's my opinion that items such as this (and some companies stretch the "exempt" type of times to great limits), remove the urgency from minimizing this type of activity; you're lessening the need to ensure that these activities are conducted at a high level of efficiency. So, why not include them in OEE*

calculations and strive to remove all waste from these activities? Isn't that what being Lean is about – understanding your current performance and continuously improving it? Isn't that common sense?

I contend that OEE was intended to be an analytic metric that helps companies identify opportunities for improvement by setting an accurate baseline and then relentless striving to improve it. But when you start seeing companies use OEE as a management / employee performance metric, then people start to play games with it – e.g. exempt certain activities (that take availability away from production), increase batch sizes to minimize change-overs, misstate the theoretical performance of a machine, etc. It can drive the wrong behaviors.

Additionally, OEE is really a good measure for process manufacturing or elements of the semiconductor industry and piece equipment for which the true quality of output is not known until much later in the process, thereby "ignoring" the quality component of the OEE calculation. Not really know-ing the quality level of a semiconductor wafer's die until it's probed much later in the process doesn't easily allow you to link quality to a single piece of equipment. So, OEE may be a good metric to identify opportunities for improvement in the availability and performance components of OEE, but not necessarily the quality aspect.

I make / share these observations to get you thinking about how OEE can be an effective metric for your organization to think about some of the poten-tial pitfalls.

Another OEE-related metric is TEEP (Total Effective Equipment Performance). TEEP is an absolute measurement of the utilization of an asset. TEEP calculates your performance based on 24 hours/days and 365 days/year; it is considered to be a measure of a facility's true capacity (Figure 3.38).

■ Loading = Scheduled Time / Calendar Time
  – If production is scheduled to run 21 hours/day (3 hours of breaks/ meals), 5 days/week, then Loading = (21 hours/day × 5 days) ÷ (24 hours/day × 7 days) = 62.5%.
■ Loading is also known as overall facility utilization.

TEEP: (Total Effective Equipment Performance)	
=	Loading x Overall Equipment Effectiveness (OEE)

Figure 3.38 Total Effective Equipment Performance.

NEE: (Net Equipment Effectiveness)	
=	Uptime (UT) x Performance Efficiency x Rate of Quality (RA)

Figure 3.39 Net Equipment Effectiveness.

Another OEE-related metric is NEE (net equipment effectiveness). NEE is very similar to the TEEP but simpler, as it takes into account pure equipment uptime regardless of planned downtime; it only captures that the equipment is running and producing parts. The uptime of the equipment is denoted as UT. The other two components of the calculation are performance efficiency (PE), which is calculated same as OEE's performance (P), and rate of quality (RA), which is calculated same as OEE's quality (Q) (Figure 3.39).

Case-in-Point Example 3.14 Machine FMEA

FMEA (Failure Mode and Effect Analysis) will be covered in detail in the Total Quality Management section, and I can tell you in advance that I am a big fan of the tool and methodology. This case story reflects the application of the Machine FMEA (MFMEA) within TPM's focus on the total-life management of equipment, especially the management of new equipment acquisitions.

The MFMEA (a.k.a. Equipment FMEA (EFMEA) or Machine Design FMEA (MDFMEA)) utilizes the conventional FMEA methodology for evaluating equipment and tooling during its design phase to improve operator safety, reliability, and robustness of the machinery. The use of a MFMEA for this purpose has slowly started to gain traction. This case story reflects the application of the MFMEA being expanded to cover newly transferred (received) or modified / overhauled or poorly performing equipment (equipment, machinery, and tooling). The MFMEA is applied to production, laboratory, and facility equipment, machinery, or tooling).

The MFMEA is beneficial in

■ improving safety, reliability, and robustness of equipment / tooling;
■ allowing any potential design changes to be incorporated early, including design changes that could positively or negatively affect operational safety, quality, delivery, and/or cost;
■ spare parts planning;
■ minimizing new equipment, machinery, or tooling procurement costs and delivery delays;
■ reducing the overall life-cycle costs of the equipment, machinery, or tooling.

Failure Mode and Effects Analysis (Machine FMEA)

Item: ____________ Responsibility: ____________ FMEA Number: ____________

Key Date (Orig): ____________ Date Revised: ____________ Prepared By: ____________

Core Team: ____________

Equipment or Machinery (or Sub-system) Name	Function and Performance Requirement	Potential Failure Mode (s)	Potential Effect(s) of Failure	Severity	Classification	Potential Cause(s) / Mechanisms of Failure	Occurrence	Current Design Controls and Machinery Cotrols	Detection	RPN	Recommended Action	Responsibility & Target Completion Date	Action Results				
													Actions Taken - Completion Date	Severity	Occurrence	Detection	RPN

Figure 3.40 Example – Machine FMEA.

The MFEA used is this case story is shown in Figure 3.40. It contains only minor variations from a standard FMEA, with some headings altered slightly to be more reflective of an equipment, machinery, or tooling FMEA rather than a process- or product-related one.

The major difference between MFMEA and any other type of FMEA is the criteria for the elements of your Risk Priority Number, i.e. severity, occurrence, and detection.

Figure 3.41a–c shows examples utilized for a MFMEA.

The facility has seen a continuous increase in its OEE for new and existing production and facility equipment, which is partially attributable to the deployment of the MFMEA on ALL new equipment and for other key (or critical) equipment.

Case-in-Point Example 3.15 Overall Equipment Effectiveness (Medical Device Manufacturer)

The scenario for this case story was the packaging line for a medical device manufacturer. The piece of equipment with a low OEE was an automatic laminating and sealing machine, which was a part of a sequential continuous flow packaging line. These machines had an OEE in the mid-40s (%), mainly because the availability was in the low-60s (%). This equipment was in a GMP (Good Manufacturing Practices) where there were strict line-clearance processes for product changeover; so, the perception was that the low OEE was attributable to lost availability due to frequent product changes requiring a complete purging of all product-related material from the full line. As

Effect	Severity Criteria	Ranking
Hazardous without Warning	Very high severity. Affects operator, facility or maintenance personnel. Effects safety and/or non-compliant with government regulations.	10
Hazardous with Warning	Very high severity. Affects operator, facility or maintenance personnel. Effects safety and/or non-compliant with government regulations.	9
Very High Downtime or Defective Parts	Downtime of more than 8-hours or a DPM > xxx	8
Very High Downtime or Defective Parts	Downtime of >4 & ≤8-hours or a xxx > DPM ≤ xxx	7
Moderate Downtime or Defective Parts	Downtime of >1 & ≤4-hours or a xxx > DPM ≤ xxx	6
Low Downtime or Defective Parts	Downtime of >0.5 & ≤1-hour or a 0 > DPM ≤ xxx	5
Very Low Downtime & No Defective Parts	Downtime of ≥0.5-hour or a DPM of 0.	4
Minor Effect	Process parameters variability outside control limits; adjustments required. No defective parts.	3
Very Minor Effect	Process parameters variability within control limits; adjustments required. No defective parts.	2
No Effect	Process parameters variability within control limits; no adjustments required. No defective parts.	1

Probability of Failure Occurrence	Possible Failure Rates	Ranking
Very High Failure is Almost Inevitable	Intermittent operation resulting in 1 failure in ≤10 production pieces or MTBF < 1-hour	10
	Intermittent operation resulting in 10 <1 failure ≤100 production pieces or 1≤ MTBF < 10-hours	9
High: Repeated Failures	Intermittent operation resulting in 100 <1 failure ≤1,000 production pieces or 10≤ MTBF < 100-hrs	8
	Intermittent operation resulting in 1,000 <1 failure ≤10,000 production pcs or 100≤ MTBF < 400-hrs	7
Moderate: Occasional Failures	400≤ MTBF < 1,000-hrs	6
	1,000≤ MTBF < 2,000-hrs	5
	2,000≤ MTBF < 3,000-hrs	4
Low: Relatively few Failures	3,000≤ MTBF < 6,000-hrs	3
	6,000≤ MTBF < 10,000-hrs	2
Remote: Failure Unlikely	10,000≤ MTBF	1

Figure 3.41 Risk Priority Number – Examples : (a) Severity scoring criteria, (b) Occurrence scoring criteria, (c) Detection scoring criteria.

we analyzed the availability data through the pareto of lost availability, we learned that product changeovers were significant but that this was not the area of the largest loss. The largest time loss was due to preventive maintenance (PM). PM was allocated eight hours of downtime, but the data revealed that they actually took significantly longer. So, we conducted a kaizen to review the PM processes. The initial step was to video an actual PM; the result of the video was that the majority of PM downtime was due to technicians searching for tools and, inevitably, having to make multiple trips to the spare-parts storeroom for miscellaneous parts. The kaizen resulted in the creation

Detection	Likelihood of Detection by Design or Machine Control	Ranking
Absolute Uncertainty	Machine controls will not and/or cannot detect potential cause / mechanism and subsequent failure mode; or these is no design or machine control.	10
Very Remote	Very remote chance a machine or design control will detect a potential cause / mechanism and subsequent failure mode	9
Remote	Remote chance a machine / design control will detect a potential cause /mechanism and subsequent failure mode. Machine control will prevent an imminent failure.	8
Very Low	Very low chance a machine / design control will detect a potential cause /mechanism and subsequent failure mode. Machine control will prevent an imminent failure	7
Low	Low chance a machine / design control will detect a potential cause /mechanism and subsequent failure mode. Machine control will prevent an imminent failure	6
Moderate	Moderate chance a machine / design control will detect a potential cause /mechanism and subsequent failure mode. Machine control will prevent an imminent failure and will isolate the cause. Machinery control may be required.	5
Moderate High	Moderately high chance a machine / design control will detect a potential cause /mechanism and subsequent failure mode. Machine control will prevent an imminent failure and will isolate the cause. Machinery control may be required.	4
High	High chance a machine / design control will detect a potential cause /mechanism and subsequent failure mode. Machine control will prevent an imminent failure and will isolate the cause. Machinery control may be required.	3
Very High	Very high chance a machine / design control will detect a potential cause /mechanism and subsequent failure mode. Machinery control not required.	2
Almost Certain	Design control will almost certainly detect a potential cause / mechanism and subsequent failure mode. Machinery control not required.	1

Figure 3.41   (Continued)

of a standardized PM cart that had all necessary tools and the most common spare parts; everything was arranged on the cart in a shadow board-type arrangement so that it was easy to ensure that everything was available before stopping the machine (using a SMED technique for PM, i.e. moving previous internal activities to external). The kaizen team also devised a detailed standardized work of the key PM steps and included a checklist to ensure the steps were performed in the most efficient sequence. The overall result was that the PMs were reduced to less than four hours; availability was raised to the mid-80s (%) and the OEE was raised from the mid-40s to the mid-60s.

Additional steps were taken to optimize the line-clearance processes; our analysis of the OEE revealed that we had considerable losses due to performance (P) being affected by minor machine stoppages; our comprehensive analysis linked these back to machine components that needed to be replaced more frequently. These tasks were added to the PM checklists.

After a few months of improvements, the OEE was increased to the mid-70s (%), which was a great accomplishment, especially considering that this facility had more than 20 of these packaging machines.

Total Quality Management

Total Quality Management (TQM) is a term that refers comprehensively to the many tools and methodologies related to quality control and other aspects of quality.

TQM is a management approach to long-term success through obtaining customer satisfaction. In a TQM environment, all associates of an organization participate in improving the processes, products, and/or services and embracing the enterprise's Lean and quality culture.

There are very strong synergies in the TQM principles and the "principles" of both Lean and Six Sigma. Some of the TQM principles (per American Society for Quality) include:

■ being customer-focused;
■ total employee involvement;
■ being process center focused;
■ integrated system (focused on the horizontal processes that run across functions);
■ strategic and systematic approach (reference the X-Matrix);
■ continual improvement;
■ fact-based (and data-driven) decision making;
■ communication.

There are a few tools that are consider the basics of quality (or quality control); the origin of this terminology is typically related to the post-World War II (circa 1950s) quality revolution in Japan emphasized by Dr. Kaoru Ishikawa (a Japanese professor) and is based heavily on the teachings of Dr. Edward Deming (an American engineer, professor, management consultant, etc.). These tools are simple graphical and statistical techniques that can be utilized in solving quality-related issues.

Dr. Ishikawa is also credited with the introduction of quality circles and as the creator of the Ishikawa diagram (a.k.a. fishbone or cause-and-effect diagram).

These are the tools that you should master along your transformation journey.

Please note that over the years there have been minor variations on what comprises the seven tools, but below I'm listing the ones that I most often seen linked to the basic seven quality tools and that I feel can be the most beneficial in your Lean journey.

TQM's Seven (7) Basic Quality Tools

1. **Flow Charts**
   – This is a visual diagram of how the process being investigated operates.
   – In Lean, this is easily expanded to include Value Stream Mapping.
2. **Cause-and-Effect Diagram** (a.k.a. Fishbone Diagram and/or Ishikawa Diagram)
   – This a tool for systematically arranging the results of an effect with the factors (causes) that influence it.
   – It is a method of brainstorming the possible causes of a problem or situation.
   – A problem or effect is defined, and its possible causes are brainstormed. Brainstorming must be unconstrained; there are no stupid or bad suggestions.
   – Hint: The categories of causes are typically man, machine, method, measurement, materials, and Mother Nature (or environment), but the category titles are unimportant; they only serve as a thought/idea enabler.

This is a tool that I believe can be the most powerful tool in your quality toolbox, but you must master the skill of facilitating the exercise. Keys to facilitation including drawing out as many potential root causes

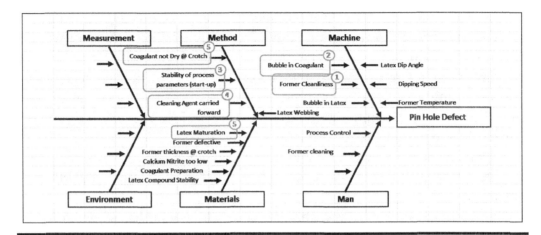

Figure 3.42   Example of an effective fishbone diagram.

as possible (no bad ideas) and having a very open brainstorming environment in which everyone is equal.

Figure 3.42 shows an example of a successful fishbone diagram. The items circled in red are the results of the "potential root-cause" voting by the brainstorming participants. For the top three vote-getters, there would be another one or two layers of fishbone diagraming (or possibly a 5-Whys progression).

3. **Check Sheets**
   - This arranges data by type.
   - It is a method of recording factual data over a period of time.
   - A check sheet confirms (or contradicts) causes of the problem.
   - It is primarily utilized at a workstation or piece of equipment (Figure 3.43).

Operation time	Defect 1 Dirty	Defect 2 Scratched	Defect 3 Missing punch	Defect 4 Double punch	Defect 5 Off center
Date 7-9AM	11111	1		111	11111
Date 9-11AM	1	111	1	111	11111
Date 11AM-1PM	111	1		111111111	1111
Date 1-3PM		1	1	111	111

Figure 3.43   Example of a check-sheet.

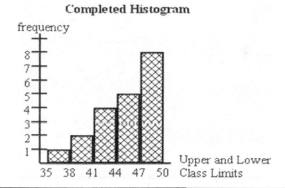

Figure 3.44   Example of a histogram.

4. Histogram

– This is a method to allow data collected from a process over a period of time (reflects the frequency of an occurrence).
– The resulting display can show relative frequency of occurrences, process centering, and the shape of the distribution of the data, indicate process center shifts, and answer basic questions around process capability (Figure 3.44).

5. Pareto Charts

– This is a method of showing a table of data in a graphical format to aid understanding. It classifies problems and defects by type in the order of quantities and the cumulative total.
– It plots the Pareto results in descending order, with categories on the horizontal axis and % frequency of occurrence on the vertical axis.
– A Pareto chart highlights the "vital few" vs. the "trivial many" (Figure 3.45).

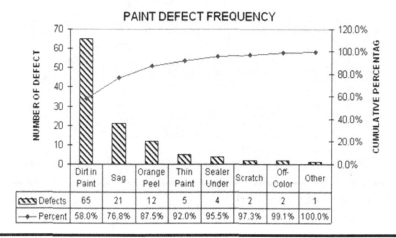

Figure 3.45   Example of a Pareto chart.

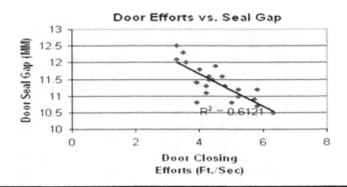

Figure 3.46 Example of a scatter diagram.

6. Scatter Diagram

– This is a method of analysis used to quantify the relationship between two or more input variables (X) and an output variable(s) (Y). It establishes if there's a correlation between variables (but correlation doesn't necessarily mean causation; you'll need to validate) (Figure 3.46).

7. Control Charts

– These are statistical charts used to continuously monitor and provide information about the performance of a process.
– They are used to monitor and control the performance of new processes.
– They identify common cause vs. special cause variations (Figure 3.47).

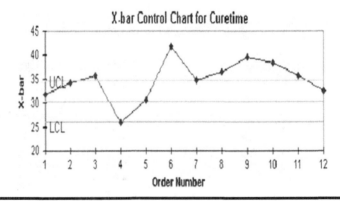

Figure 3.47 Example of a control chart.

5-Whys

5-Whys is not listed as one of the basic quality tools, but it is one of the most used tools in problem solving today. 5-Whys is an iterative interrogative technique to explore the cause-and-effect relationship of a problem and its potential causes. The coining of the terminology, 5-Whys, is often credited to Taiichi Ohno (of Toyota fame). The 5-Whys technique has often been proclaimed as the backbone of Toyota's Quality System; at the very least, it is recognized as a problem solving technique widely used by Toyota production associates.

The technique is very simple: Repeat the question "why" until the you've identified the root cause. The answer for one question forms the basis for the next question (Figure 3.48).

The reason why "5" is the number of iterations that you should ask a question to determine the root cause of a problem is very anecdotal, as there no scientific proof that five and only five repetitions of "why" will definitely identify the true root cause; it is, however, definitely a rule-of-thumb to follow. The point is that you must ask "why" until you feel that you have exhausted the potential stream of causes for a problem, whether that's five iterations or three or seven.

The 5-Whys technique has a potential major flaw, as it is subject to the validity of the answers and the number of iterations that you undertake. The 5-Whys technique is very dependent on the knowledge and persistence of the people involved.

I have seen many forms designed to assist in the 5-Whys process. The ones that I like are the ones that have a simple (but subjective) validation built in, that after a root cause has been established, you backtrack the whys by inserting "therefore" between answers of the questions to see if they make logical sense (i.e. common sense).

Figure 3.48 demonstrates a 5-Whys format that I think provides a solid platform for utilizing the 5-Whys technique.

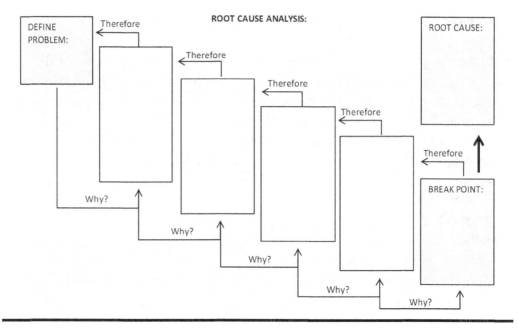

Figure 3.48   Example of a 5-Whys diagram (a.k.a. Root Cause Analysis diagram).

Case-in-Point Example 3.16 5-Whys and the Jefferson Memorial (Figure 3.49)

This case story is not from one of my personal experiences, but it is an example of 5-Whys that is easy to comprehend and does a good job of demonstrating the technique. I have personally tried to verify the veracity

Figure 3.49   The Jefferson Memorial & 5-Whys.

of this situation and have found archived newspaper articles documenting this situation (this event happened before the internet was in existence and before "fake news" became a tagline), so I'm taking it as a true sequence of activities.

The scenario was that the Jefferson Memorial (Washington, DC) required regular pressure-washings due the build-up of bird poop on the exterior of the memorial; these regular pressure-washings were deteriorating the surface of the memorial. So, a team of memorial caretakers tried to determine how to minimize the accumulation of bird poop on the memorial.

There were some quick solutions that were just as quickly eliminated, such as:

- simply kill all the birds – but that would not be a politically correct solution, and it's probably not even feasible to kill all the birds;
- blast loud music to deter the birds from congregating on the memorial's roof – but that would also be a deterrent to the masses of tourists that consistently visit the memorial, and not having tourists enjoying the memorial defeats the purpose of having a memorial;
- build a spiked structure to prohibit the birds from landing on the roof – but that would also largely distract from the aesthetic appeal of the memorial. Tourists often go to the memorials to take photographs (selfies) or to just sit and enjoy its beauty, so a metal structure massive enough to protect the memorial from the birds would be an unsightly addition to the memorial, most likely at an extremely high and unjustifiable cost;

So, luckily, the powers-that-be decided to take a more systematic approach and try to identify the root cause for the birds congregating on the roof of the memorial and decorating it with their poop. So, they went through a 5-Whys technique:

- The Jefferson Memorial requires excessive power washes. Why?
- Because birds are swarming to the monument and depositing large amounts of droppings. Why?
- Because they are feeding on an unusually large numbers of spiders living under the roof line. Why?
- Because the spiders are feeding on an unusually high number of midge flies as they hatch throughout the day. Why?
- Because midge fly larvae are literally caked under the roof line of the memorial. Why?
- Because the midge flies were attracted to the memorial. Why?
- It turns out, the lights that illuminate the memorial were set to come on automatically 20 minutes before dusk; this twilight condition created an ideal condition for midge flies to mate.

Solution: The automatic lights were re-set to reduce the twilight condition. This solution worked; therefore, there were fewer midge flies; therefore, there was less larvae and fewer spiders; therefore, there were fewer birds; therefore, there was less poop; therefore, fewer pressure-washings were required.

Just as an interesting side note, my research showed that this was a true series of events and that the solution was effective; however, I found articles stating that the solution was abandoned shortly after its implementation as many of the photographers that frequently visited the memorial around dusk did so because of the great photographic opportunities created by the sun at dusk and the memorial's illumination. So, they strongly protested the elimination of this perfect photographic experience, and thus, the powers-that-be decided to revert to the old illumination settings and continue with the frequent washings (maybe less frequent).

So, as I stated at the start, whether this is 100% factual or not, this example is a great and effective utilization of the 5-Whys technique.

The 5-Whys and the seven basic quality tools are the prime tools for conducting a Root Cause Analysis (RCA). In most situations, to derive the definitive root cause, a combination of tools and methodologies is required (Figure 3.50).

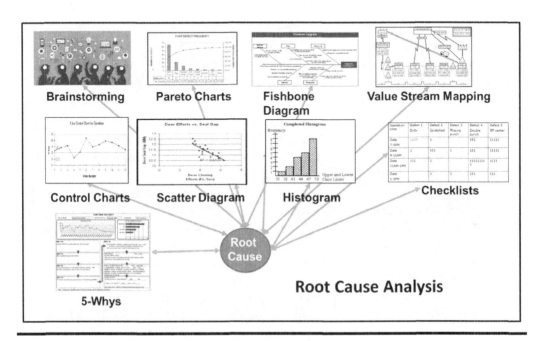

Figure 3.50 Root Cause Analysis tools & methodologies.

Case-in-Point Example 3.17 Root Cause Analysis

The scenario for this Root Cause Analysis was that a medical device forming line was realizing a high level of defects, so a tiger team (a.k.a. task force) was established to reduce the defect levels.

The initial step was to create a pareto of defects. From the pareto, it was determined that the largest occurrence of defects was the result of "crotch pinhole" defects (i.e. a very small hole in the adjoining fingers area of a latex glove). So, with a cross-functional group of subject matter experts, I facilitated the creation of a fishbone diagram (Figure 3.51).

After brainstorming for several minutes, it was determined that we had exhausted identifying potential causes of the pinhole defect. So, to determine the most likely potential root cause of pinholes, I asked the participants to vote for their choice of the most likely potential root cause. I allowed everyone to place three votes, and they could split their votes any way they chose. This was an open verbal vote; however, sometimes it may be best to have a silent vote to ensure no prejudices or peer pressure. The consensus of the participants' votes was that "former cleanliness" was the most likely root cause of the pinhole defect.

So, the next step was to brainstorm and conduct a fishbone diagram of "former cleanliness". The resulting fishbone is shown in Figure 3.52.

So, after another session of voting by the participants, the top three potential causes of "former cleanliness" were identified. The top three potential root causes (actually four, as there was a tied vote) were then individually subjected to a 5-Whys analysis. One common cause was identified, which was inconsistencies in the performance of some key process checks: former temperature, line speed, pH of cleaning agent, chemical levels, brush preventative maintenance frequency, improper former handling, etc.; all could be traced back to human error. So, we did a simple

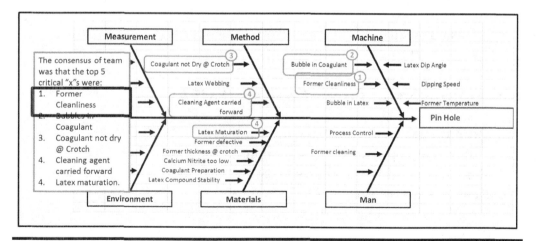

Figure 3.51 Case-in-Point Example 3.17 Root Cause Analysis: Fishbone diagram level 1.

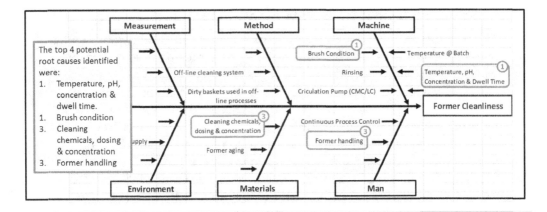

Figure 3.52 Case-in-Point Example 3.17 Root Cause Analysis: Fishbone diagram level 2.

Root Cause Analysis of the human error and found that the causes of human error were no Standard Work and insufficient training. The solution was to create Standard Work in the forms of checklists and visual aids. The visual aids were process steps with pictures to highlight the key job elements. Visual aids were added to the actual forming line, such as max–min levels of chemicals, digital temperature gauges, and line-audit checklists.

Improvement in the defect levels was obtained; so, we then repeated the cause-and-effect steps for the second highest ranked potential causes and then repeated these sequences until we felt that we had exhausted all improvement ideas. At that point, we moved on to the second highest occurring defect (back to the Pareto chart).

The Root Cause Analysis process is continuous improvement process; eliminate root causes one by one and then continue on to the next potential root cause or the next defect category as identified by the Pareto chart.

We thus institutionalized a system of continuous defect reduction.

Failure Mode and Effect Analysis (FMEA)

FMEA can be one of the most powerful tools of TQM ... or Lean ... or Six Sigma. But in my opinion, it's vastly underutilized.

Failure Mode and Effect Analysis (FMEA) is a step by step approach for identifying the risk of potential failures in a:

- design;
- product;

- manufacturing or supply chain process;
- service;
- analysis of a new or modified piece of equipment, machinery, or tooling (a Machine FMEA).

"Failure Mode" refers to the way that something might potentially fail. "Failures" can be any potential or actual errors. "Effects Analysis" refers to understanding the potential consequences of those failures.

You should consider conducting a FMEA when:

- a process, product, or service is being designed or redesigned (modified);
- an existing process, product, or service is being applied in a new way;
- developing a control plan for a new or modified process;
- improvement goals are planned for an existing process, product, or service (i.e. a FMEA for a value stream improvement);
- analyzing failures of an existing process, product, or service (a potential reverse-FMEA by starting with potential failure, an effect, and working backward through the process);
- periodically throughout the life of the process, product, or service;
- purchasing or modifying a piece of equipment or machinery or tooling.

Figure 3.53 shows an example of a FMEA template.

The same "basic" process is followed for any type of FMEA (except a reverse-FMEA).

Process / Product
Failure Modes and Effects Analysis Form
(FMEA)

Process or Product Name:		Prepared by:	Page ___ of ___
Responsible:		FMEA Date (Orig) ___________ (Rev) ___________	

Process Step / Input	Potential Failure Mode	Potential Failure Effects	SEVERITY	Potential Causes	OCCURRENCE	Current Controls	DETECTION	RPN	Actions Recommended	Resp.	Actions Taken	SEVERITY	OCCURRENCE	DETECTION	RPN
What is the process step and Input under investigation?	In what ways does the Key Input go wrong?	What is the impact on the Key Output Variables (Customer Requirements)?		What causes the Key Input to go wrong?		What are the existing controls and procedures (inspection and test) that prevent either the cause or the Failure Mode?			What are the actions for reducing the occurrence of the cause, or improving detection?		What are the completed actions taken with the recalculated RPN?				

Figure 3.53 Example of a FMEA template.

Here are the components of a Process FMEA:

- listed process steps;
- potential failure mode (to be determined via brainstorming with upstream and downstream stakeholders and process owners);
- potential failure effects;
- rating the severity of potential failures;
- potential cause of failure;
- probability that a failure will occur (probability of occurrence);
- assess current process controls;
- rate the probability that a failure would be detected;
- calculate the RPN (Risk Priority Number: Severity × Occurrence × Detection):
  - best possible RPN score (lowest risk) = 1
  - worst possible RPN score (highest risk) = 1,000
- recommended actions;
- responsible person and target date;
- actions taken;
- new severity rating (scores);
- new severity rating (scores);
- new severity rating (scores);
- new (projected) RPN.

The components listed in Figure 3.53 represent a Process FMEA; a Product FMEA is similar, but instead of process steps in the first column, you would substitute product functions. For a Machine FMEA, you'd substitute process steps for equipment functionality.

A couple of important notes:

- There is no targeted RPN score. The key is that you prioritize your countermeasures by attacking the highest RPNs first. Additionally, the RPN establishes a baseline so that you can determine if your countermeasures are effective.
- A key to a great FMEA is the establishment of the criteria on how you'll rank an item in terms of severity, occurrence, and detection; if possible, make the criteria quantitative rather than subjective. Create the criteria with a cross-functional team – the same team that will complete the FMEA.

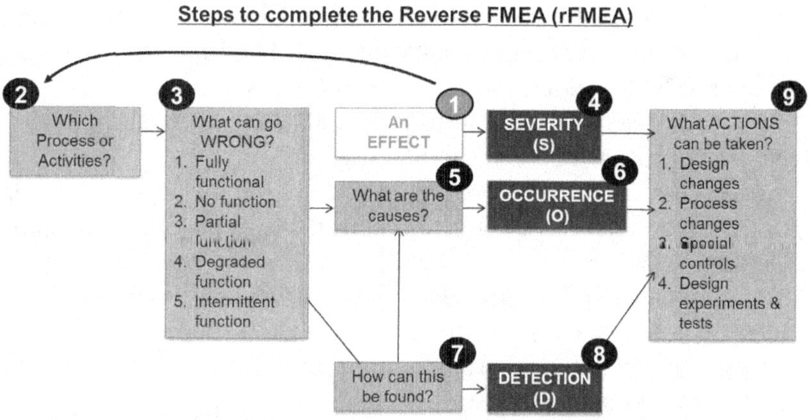

Steps to complete the Reverse FMEA (rFMEA)

Figure 3.54   Process steps in conducting a reverse-FMEA (rFMEA).

One of my favorite FMEA applications is the reverse-FMEA (or rFMEA). You would use the rFMEA if you have a known failure effect, and you want to backtrack and assess a process to identify all potential causes. The case story below highlights an rFMEA application.

The typical steps to completing a rFMEA are shown in the diagram in Figure 3.54.

Case-in-Point Example 3.18 Reverse-FMEA

This case story happened at an American electronic component manufacturer in Asia. The company was seeing a large variance in the amount of raw material that was supposed to be used by production (bill of material standard versus area product-completed data) versus the "actual" usage, based on the daily ERP backflush for this production area. The daily variance had grown exponentially and was far exceeding the "shrinkage" standard for this product line. This variance is assumed to be a defect (i.e. scrap). The manager of this product line was sure that the material wasn't really scrapped, but he was equally unsure of what might be causing the increasing variance.

When I was approached with this scenario, I immediately instructed the team to conduct a rFMEA, but the team was reluctant as they were sure that only one process step was the root cause of the increasing variance. But at my insistence, I led the team through a rFMEA.

The shrinkage standard (production loss) that had been built into the costing of the product was <1,000 pieces/day, but the actual variance was at that time > 100,000/day.

So, the initial action was to develop a rFMEA. The steps were as follows:

1. Assemble a cross-functional team (horizontal and vertical) of "stake-holders" (if not identified as a stakeholder, then process/quality engineers should be added as subject matter experts to the team);
2. On a FMEA form, add the "effect" (e.g. Material xx Variance);
3. Fill in all process steps on the FMEA form;
4. Proceed through each process step and determine (group consensus) of the severity (S) if the "effect" occurred at this process step (step #1);
5. Determine (group consensus) what would be the possible Failure Modes to cause the default "effect" at this process step (step #1);
6. Identify potential causes of the Failure Mode (group consensus);
7. Determine (group consensus) the frequency for this cause to occur (O) at this process step (step #1);
8. Determine (group consensus) the likelihood of the cause to be detected (D) at this step (step #1);
9. Calculate the Risk Priority Number (RPN) $[RPN = S \times O \times D]$;
10. Repeat these steps for all remaining process steps;
11. After completing the mode and effect analysis for all steps, and based on the highest RPNs, start developing countermeasures to eliminate the causes [limited initial countermeasure focuses to the top three highest RPNs];
12. brainstorm and implement countermeasures, then recalculate RPNs and repeat Step 11 again … and again … and again.

The team followed the above steps and was able to identify 18 causes with RPNs ranging from 576 to 80. So, the team had identified 18 possible causes, rather than one as originally thought. But to the team's credit, the root cause that they had previously assumed was the only cause did result in the highest RPN (576).

The team uncovered many other improvement opportunities from this rFMEA initiative, and many of the causes identified were resolved by simple quick-win activities.

After the team addressed the top seven RPN causes, the daily variance was reduced to < 500.

Workplace Organization (5S + Safety)

I try to refrain from using the terminology of 6S; for 5S, I prefer to call it workplace organization (WO). The focus on safety should not be diluted by workplace organization activities. But that's just my opinion.

I'd be surprised if anyone reading this book weren't well educated on the basis of 5S, but I'll cover some of the highlights here.

■ 5S is derived from five Japanese terms, which are translated (or interpreted) into English as:
  – Sort;
  – Set-in-Order;
  – Shine;
  – Standardize;
  – Sustain.

5S is most often thought of as a housekeeping initiative, and in most instances, that's how 5S is deployed (i.e. as a housekeeping initiative). But for 5S to be effective, it must be perceived as much more than just a house-keeping exercise.

■ Sort, the first S, is about removing unnecessary items from the workplace (both factory and office). This is definitely a great practice to follow. The "golden rule" of Sort is that if you don't have an immediate need for it, then sort it out.
  – A key mechanism of Sort is the Red Tag process. Red Tagging is applying a Red Tag to any item in an area that is found to be unnecessary, inoperable, or status unknown. An item is to be Red Tagged and then moved to a Red Tag Area to be held for dispositioning. The time allowed for an item to be held in the Red Tag Area varies from weeks to months; I prefer a maximum of two weeks.
■ The second S is Set-in-Order. The focus needs to be on Set-in-Order, i.e. workplace organization. Set-in-Order is more than just removing clutter from the workplace; it's arranging material equipment, workstations, product, etc. in a sequence that follows the flow of the process.
  – The workplace organization should be aligned to minimize muda (pure waste, a.k.a. TIMWOOD), muri (overburdening), and mura (unevenness).
  – The workplace should be organized to:
    • minimize transportation (eliminate excessive handling and transporting of material and product);
    • reduce (eliminate) inventory and maintain the proper Standard WIP (SWIP);

- optimize the principles of motion (optimize and promote proper ergonomics);
- promote uninterrupted flow, eliminating waiting;
- make any overproduction visible and maintain the proper Standard WIP (SWIP);
- ensure an efficient workplace that supports the elimination of over-processing (hand-offs, re-handling, etc.);
- minimize defects by promoting uninterrupted flow and minimizing handling, etc.

The workplace organization must promote the elimination of muri (overburdening); an efficient workplace exhibits adherence to the principles of motion and the ergonomically optimized environment.

A well-organized workplace will promote uninterrupted flow of information, material, product, and people, resulting in a balanced workload and thus the elimination of muda (unevenness).

The litmus test or the effectiveness of your Set-in-Order effort is the 30-second test. Within 30 seconds, anyone should be able to walk into your area and determine if it is operating/performing as expected or identify noticeable abnormalities.

■ The third S is Shine. Shine is about a deep cleaning of an area, e.g. sweep, dust, polish, and paint.

I think the best analogy of the benefit of Shine is to compare it to washing your car. Think back; as you're washing your car, you notice every nick, scratch, ding, etc. So, you end up with a clean car, but you've also noticed any new blemishes, etc.; now, you must devise a plan to address those blemishes (e.g. buff out, re-paint, leave as-is, etc.).

So, during the Shine of your area, you'll want to identify the causes of the dirt and grime and eliminate them. The focus of Shine should be removing the need to clean.

■ The fourth S is Standardize. Standardize is about establishing the system to sustain your workplace organization and its cleanliness.
Standardizing 5S is about:
- establishing an area cleaning schedule (daily, weekly, monthly, and quarterly) – who, what, when, and how?
- establishing an audit process and procedure. Who, what, when, and how?

■ The fifth and final S is Sustain. This is the most difficult part of a 5S program – sustaining the gains.

A few items that can support your effort to sustain:

– Implement a Code of Conduct:
  • if you open it, close it;
  • if you borrow it, return it;
  • if you make a mess, clean it up;
  • if you moved it, put it back;
  • Etc.
– Create a "5S corner" in every area – an area to store 5S supplies, for 5S information, etc.;
– Create a 5S Checklist – a checklist of key items to be checked on a regular basis;
– Create a 5S patrol – a 5S audit team of rotating associates;
– Create a steering committee – a cross-functional team to set the direction of the 5S program;
– Enforce 5S Gemba Walks – regularly scheduled leadership (senior management) walks with a focus on 5S;
– Create a 5S audit program – a tiered audit program, e.g. self, associates, area owners, supervisors, managers, site leaders, and/or steering committee;
– Encourage 5S competition – monthly or quarterly competition between departments (factory and office);
– Create a visual coordinator who provides 5S support in terms of subject matter expertise, training, and activity coordination;
– Create a management champion – an executive of high standing to support the 5S program.

Case-in-Point Example 3.19 My 5S Fail (Medical Device Manufacturer in Thailand)

When I started my role of Director of Operational Excellence in an American company's manufacturing facility in Thailand, one item that caught my early attention was the monthly 5S competition.

There was a steering committee that performed monthly audits of all factory and office areas and awarded prizes for the best area for the factory and the office area. They also awarded a "worst"-place trophy for the worst areas. The "best" area received a floating trophy and also (most importantly to the associates) free ice cream for all members of the winning areas.

To me, the awarding of ice cream was childish, with no real benefit. Their paycheck should be enough of a "reward" along with the public recognition of being a member of the award-winning area/team.

So, I halted the awarding of the ice cream treat with the support of the upper management (also Western expatriates like myself).

The results? In one swoop, I destroyed almost everyone's motivation to keep their areas clean and organized. Our overall plantwide 5S started falling off almost immediately; the competition (with an ice cream reward) was a motivator to maintain a 5S compliance area. After realizing my error, I reinstated the "ice cream rewards", but the damage that I created took a long time to overcome. Eventually, however, the 5S regained traction.

I started using ice cream as a motivator in many different areas to gain immediate support. The Thais enjoy their ice cream!

And, finally, because of my original resistance to the "ice cream rewards", my department was infamously awarded the "worst" department award for three months in a row until I disbanded the "worst" trophy, as I really didn't think the negativity of a "worst" award was the culture that I wanted to cultivate. The "ice cream award" was reinstated, but the "worst" trophy stayed retired (the trophy was still in my office 2+ years later when I departed on my next adventure).

Case-in-Point Example 3.20 Red Tag Abuse (Electronics Manufacturer in Asia)

The scenario of this case story is that I joined a manufacturing company in Asia that had a long-standing 6S program that had implemented Red Tagging many years earlier.

I became aware of the existing Red Tagging policy as I joined the weekly Gemba Walks, as I noticed Red Tagged items throughout the production and office areas.

There were also designated Red Tag Areas in the production area.

In my Gemba Walks, I continued to notice the proliferation of Red Tagged items – under workstations, under office desks, utilized by production associates, in storage/staging areas, etc. But the incident that finally caught my heightened disdain was seeing non-conforming material being Red Tagged – and, more importantly, not being quarantined.

My immediate investigation revealed that Red Tags were placed on anything in an area that wasn't immediately being used, but the items weren't relocated to the Red Tag Area, nor were there any plans (or perceived need) to move the items out of the production or office area. For you Monopoly game players, the Red Tags were sort of their "get out of jail free" cards; i.e. it was their reprieve of any wrongdoing. It was their "license" to do nothing.

Based on my findings, I immediately started facilitating the rewriting of our 6S procedure, particularly the Red Tag section. The Red Tag methodology is an important element of all 5S/6S programs, but it must be administered properly; the proper discipline must be instilled.

**Case-in-Point Example 3.21 Workplace
Organization Best Practices Sharing**

In the case story, I just want to share some workplace organization (5S) best practices that were implemented in an electronics manufacturer in Asia. This was a large manufacturing site with more than a thousand operators.

■ There was a monthly competition of best 6S area in the offices and factory. The areas were scored on a 1–5 scale (5 = excellent, 3 = average, and 1 = bad), and to be considered as a potential winner, a score of 4 or greater had to be achieved. If no area scored a 4 or higher, there was no winner that month. Judges were chosen from the management team with different members most months (all judges came from 6S training). Judges were assigned certain zones (multiple zones, typically two factory and two office zones each) to assess and given a ~3-day window to complete the assessment. The 6S scorecard was kept simple for the ease of the judges. There would be two office and two factory winners per month, assuming the minimal score of 4 was met. The winners were awarded a large "floating" trophy that they displayed for one month and then a smaller trophy that they retained for permanent display. Additionally, the winners were announced over the PA system, and their department photo receiving the trophies was emailed to all site staff and photos were posted on bulletin boards. The winners were already very excited and proud to receive the recognition and the awards.

■ There was a quarterly 6S auditing of all areas by a group of volunteers from all levels of staff (except managers, who are exempt). The facility was divided into three zones, with a different zone audited every month. For volunteering, the auditors were not directly financially compensated, but they were given "points" that would enhance their performance rankings, which had a positive incremental effect on their annual merit increases. The audits were conducted against a detailed audit sheet that was standard for all facilities globally. These 6S scores were part of the area owners' performance review; the target was a 4 on a 1 to 5 scale.

■ Because there was a substantial amount of subjectively in the 6S scoring, the repeatability and reproducibility of the 6S measurement system had to be assessed to ensure consistency in the 6S scoring; thereby, all "certified" auditors had to "pass" an Attribute Agreement Analysis (AAA) study.

■ There were weekly management Gemba Walks that focused on 6S. The walks were restricted to certain zones in the facilities, and all findings were documented in a log, supported by photos (taken during the walk) and weekly emails to all walk participants, area owners, and the leadership team. Eighty-five percent of all findings were expected to be resolved with two weeks; a rolling log was maintained for all "open" actions. The closure rate (> 85%) was monitored as part of the plant's metric dashboard and was included in the area owners' performance review.

Chapter 4

Selective Lean Transformation Case-in-Point Examples

Case-in-Point Example 4.1 Dynamic Inventory Model

The company in this case story was a Fast-Moving-Consumer-Goods (FMCG) (a.k.a. Consumer Packaged Goods (CPG)). The company was a global manufacturer of personal care products, household goods, etc., which meant that these products typically sold quickly and had to be replenished quickly. And if for some reason a product was sold out (no stock on the shelf), a consumer had many options from competitors' products to choose from, and/or a retailer might give the vacant shelf-space to a competing brand. So, stock-outs in a retail environment must be avoided; that's one major reason why FMCG companies are known for having the best supply chain process. This particular company was no different, as they were globally recognized for their effective supply chain. But the manufacturing site of this case story was in Indonesia, an archipelago of 10,000+ islands, which created major logistical challenges. As the fourth most populous country in the world, Indonesia was a large consumer market, but it was spread over a large area of land, with many very remote consumer areas.

The other major challenge was its product portfolio, which consisted of over 22,000 SKUs. This was a larger portfolio that most country manufacturing sites had to manage as it offered a larger range of packaging types and sizes (from individual one-use sachets to large economy family sizes).

The company had a complex distribution network that included finished-good warehouses at their three manufacturing sites, a couple of large central distribution warehouses, ten sales depots (smaller regional warehouse), and even smaller stocking locations at 11 sales offices.

The company had a global-standardized home-grown legacy ERP (Enterprise Resource Planning) system that was effective for most processes but didn't have a robust inventory management system; it wasn't set up to handle as many stocking locations as existed in Indonesia's consumer landscape. All of the above-mentioned factors made Indonesia one of the most challenging supply chains within this Fortune Global 500 company.

The ERP system did allow real-time sharing on SKU inventories at all stocking locations, and the company survived due to all of the stocking locations working together and "sharing" the inventories as needed, which was an inefficient and costly way of doing business – but they made it work.

The consulting firm that I was employed at was asked to assess their distribution strategy and develop a Microsoft Excel-based robust inventory management model.

Our assessment included:

■ gathering historical demand data for all stocking locations and an A-B-C stratification of demand at all stocking locations (the demand profiles varied significantly by geographic location);

■ calculating current-state replenishment process lead times for each SKU based on manufacturing site and current distribution strategy;

■ calculating standard deviations for demand and process lead time variations by SKUs;

■ constructing a current-state matrix of the various sales offices and current replenishment routes and transportation modes (land, sea, and both);

■ understanding existing manufacturing run strategies (frequency that SKUs are manufactured, i.e. daily, weekly, bi-weekly or monthly).

The resultants of our analysis were:

■ There were 184 SKUs that were 80% of the demand volume; we established that these SKUs must be stocked at locations and manufactured and shipped on a daily basis to minimize inventory;

■ There was a large group of SKUs (> 15,000) that we basically found to be inactive; these items would only be manufactured and shipped from factories on demand, i.e. no held inventory at any stocking location;

■ The other (approximately 5,000) SKUs would be maintained at the central distribution centers and sales depots and would be managed by maximum and minimum levels of inventories. We would statistically calculate the max–min settings for a customer service level of 98% for As (184 SKUs) and 95% for the other ~5,000 SKUs.

The company had requested (and we provided) a robust Excel inventory model, so that various scenarios could be modeled and quickly make known the impact on inventory levels. The model would recalculate new standard deviations etc. on a weekly basis and adjust the SKUs max–min as needed.

The resulting metric was a 20% reduction in the total network inventory levels, and overall transportation costs were reduced by 30%.

Case-in-Point Example 4.2 Collaborative Planning and Replenishment

This case story is for a FMCG manufacturer that wanted to improve its business processes' performance throughout its supply chain. After our assessment, the planned basis of transformation was the implementation of a Collaborative Planning and Replenishment (CPR) scheme and reengineering the business processes to support the CPR scheme.

We defined three key improvement initiatives:

1. Inventory Management and Synchronized Manufacturing
2. Consolidate Warehouses and Enhance Warehouse Management
3. Implement Demand Pull and CRP to All Sales Depots

The quantitative and qualitative results were:

1. Inventory Management and Synchronized Manufacturing
   - reduced manufacturing process lead times;
   - ~40% reduction in finished goods inventory ($3 million reduction in value);
   - reduced transportation wastes (i.e. less product handling).
2. Consolidate Warehouses and Enhance Warehouse Management
   - ~50% reduction in space;
   - elimination of the need for a third-party warehouse; saved $200K annually in rental costs;
   - ~60% reduction in transportation (transfer trips between warehouses);
   - optimized order-picking and distribution processes.
3. Implement Demand Pull and CRP to All Sales Depots
   - raised customer service level (on-time-in-full (OTIF)) from 70% to 92%;
   - improved overall responsiveness to customer requests.

Case-in-Point Example 4.3 Top Management Challenge: Optimize Business Processes Before ERP Implementation

A diversified manufacturer of consumer electronics wanted to assess current processes and reengineer as needed before implementing an ERP (SAP) system that might institutionalize present practices without enabling required performance improvements. The company has multiple factories on the same site.

The objective given by the company was to develop optimal new product introduction, order fulfillment, and supply management processes, including defined process strategy, structure, activities, resources, and infrastructure.

After our baseline assessment, the chosen improvement initiatives were:

■ standardization and simplification of core business processes across all factories;
■ implementation of a Visual Management system to replenish point-of-use kanbans;
■ analysis of current production processes and restructured production around manufacturing cells; elimination of delay and storage within the production cycle and identification of potential set-up time reduction.

The results were:	Improvement
Reduced the Order Fulfillment Process Lead-Time Time	60%
Reduce Indirect Labor (Fulltime Equivalents)	24%
Reduced Finished Goods Inventory	35%
Reduced Work-in-Process Inventory	63%
Reduced Raw Material Inventory	25%

Figure 4.1 Case-in-Point Example 4.3 transformation results.

Case-in-Point Example 4.4 Lean Transformation to Improve Competitiveness

This was a semiconductor assembly and test service provider that drastically needed to improve its overall business performance to ensure its industry competitiveness. They specifically stated that they wanted to maximize benefits while minimizing risk and disruption to their ongoing business needs.

They also requested that we train the project team members in pertinent best practices to improve the overall capabilities of the organization.

After our baseline assessment, the chosen improvement initiatives were:

■ set-up time reduction;
■ spare parts management system;
■ total productive maintenance;
■ supply management strategy and process reengineering;
■ reduction of recurring defects;
■ process lead time reduction and planning process optimization;
■ productivity improvement and manufacturing cell design.

The results were:	Improvement
Reduce the Manufacturing Process Lead-Time (average)	72%
Reduce Product Changeover Times (average)	78%
Reduced Spare Parts Inventory	43%
Improved Machine Availability	10%

Figure 4.2   Case-in-Point Example 4.4 transformation results.

Case-in-Point Example 4.5 Directive to Achieve Cost Savings without Headcount Reduction

Top management at a semiconductor assembly and test service provider had handed out a directive to identify improvement opportunities to save $750K without any headcount reduction.

Our key assessment activities were:

- create an activity-based cost model that accurately reflected the cost of non-value adding activities;
- identify cost of quality for administrative and production processes;
- use Routing By Walking Around to assess manufacturing processes (fact-based and data-driven).

Improvement initiatives included:

- simplifying five levels of planning into one by having production pull from die-bank to produce the daily production target;
- assessing manufacturing process and simulated make-to-order (pull) strategy utilizing manufacturing cells;
- formalizing plans for spare parts management and total productive maintenance;
- reclassifying purchased commodities and identifying different supply management strategies;
- assessing and suggesting improvement in material procurement cycle.

The results were:	Improvement
Reduce the Order Fulfillment Process Lead-Time (average)	45%
Reduce Equipment Set-up Times (average)	77%
Productivity Improvement	12%
Work-in-Process Inventory Reduction	50%

Figure 4.3   Case-in-Point Example 4.5 transformation results.

**Case-in-Point Example 4.6 Top Management Directive
to Optimize Order Fulfillment Processes**

Top management had made a directive to optimize the order fulfillment
processes for repetitive, discrete product manufacturing.

After completing our assessment, the improvement initiatives included:

■ eliminating engineering checking for configurable and standard models in order management cycle;

■ classifying models and developing manufacturing run strategies for
each class; moving from make-to-forecast to pull-production;

■ eliminating long planning cycle and reduced needs for re-planning by
having sales order staff check for real capacity online at order entry
and daily consolidation of orders followed by daily planning and
scheduling;

■ identifying decoupling point (supermarket) in the production process and having most materials/subassemblies pulled through the shop
floor;

■ reducing number of shop floor orders and WIP storage points.

The results were:	Improvement
Reduce the Order Fulfillment Process Lead-Time (average)	80%
Reduce Indirect Headcount	15%
Finished Goods Inventory Reduction	73%

Figure 4.4   Case-in-Point Example 4.6 transformation results.

**Case-in-Point Example 4.7 Burning Platform:
Must Improve to Survive**

After being spun-off by its parent company during a merger, this newly
independent supplier to the transportation industry needed to drastically
improve performance to ensure its survival.

What we did was:

■ design and implement manufacturing cells integrating sub-assembly,
assembly, test, and packaging;

■ implement daily scheduling (pull-production) with material replenishment by kanbans;

■ support integration of kanbans with ERP system.

The results were:	Improvement
Reduced the Order Fulfillment Process Lead-Time Time	84%
Reduce Indirect Labor (Fulltime Equivalents)	10%
Direct Labor Productivity Improvement	15%
Reduced Total Inventory	70%
Manufacturing Floor Space Reduction	60%
Reduced Average Product Changeover Times	93%

Figure 4.5   Case-in-Point Example 4.7 transformation results.

Case-in-Point Example 4.8 Maintaining Competitiveness

A manufacturer of small electric motors for consumer electronics was looking to transform its business processes in its efforts to maintain competitiveness.

The company's objectives were to

- identify opportunities for improvement;
- define optimal SAP-enabled future ways of working;
- quantify the expected benefits;
- focus the integrated implementation of new business processes and SAP on delivering measurable performance improvements.

The results obtained were:

- redefined planning strategy for build-to-order (BTO) and pull-production;
- reduced manufacturing process lead time to one day and order fulfillment process lead time to four days with build-to-order and kanban-based manufacturing strategies;
- increased manufacturing flexibility through cellular designed layout and equipment set-up reduction strategy;
- optimized finance processes in preparation for SAP implementation.

The results were:	Improvement
Reduced the Order Fulfillment Process Lead-Time Time	97%
Improve Customer Service (On-Time-In-Full)	42%
Shorten Order Entry & Customer Acknowledgement Process Lead-Time	90%
Reduce Frozen Order Window – Improve Customer Flexibility	37%

Figure 4.6   Case-in-Point Example 4.8 transformation results.

Case-in-Point Example 4.9 Implementing
a Strategic Business Review

As a result of a previously conducted Strategic Business Review (a comprehensive operational assessment), a manufacturer of residential and commercial aircon units needed to review and improve its production (including quality), planning, and procurement processes.

Its stated objective was to reduce cost and process lead times within the manufacturing, procurement, and planning areas through the introduction of industry best practices, e.g. the standardization of processes, efficiency improvements, and a reduction in inventory levels.

The results obtained were:

■ a redefined planning strategy for build-to-order (BTO) and pull-production;
■ introduction of a set-up reduction and material replenishment system using kanban to achieve a more flexible manufacturing set-up;
■ a quality system redefined and implemented into a quality-at-source scheme in its entire manufacturing environment, and extending to material suppliers.

The results were:	Improvement
Reduced the Order Fulfillment Process Lead-Time Time	53%
Reduce Equipment Set-up Times	73%
Reduce Incoming Inspection	53%
Reduce in-Process Inspection	40%
Reduce Overall Inventory	70%

Figure 4.7   Case-in-Point Example 4.9 transformation results.

Case-in-Point Example 4.10 Burning Platform Thailand

A Fast-Moving-Consumer-Goods manufacturer in Thailand had a burning platform.

Its business issues were:

■ current supply chain consisted of four central warehouses and 18 sales offices;
■ it took an average of 75 days for the product to flow through the supply chain;
■ the biggest component of supply chain costs was fixed selling expenses, followed by the cost of delivering products from sales offices to customers;
■ A service level (on-time-in-full) of 60%;

■ losing sales of almost half a billion Thai baht (US $15.9 million) a year because products were not available in the right quantities at the right place and the right time.

Our approach was:

■ complete as-is assessment and develop to-be processes and business case;
■ develop new warehouse deployment plans;
■ identify SKUs reconciliation and impact on warehouses after SKUs rationalization;
■ perform A-B-C comparison of production and sales;
■ review options for improving product flow in warehouse;
■ improve current warehouse operations:
■ re-allocate time of logistic functions;
■ reconsider warehouse layouts;
■ implement flexible manufacturing.

The results were:	Improvement
Improve Service Level (On-Time-In-Full)	>85%
Increased Inventory Turns	250%
Reduce Overall Inventory	40%
Reduce Inventory Carry Costs (annual savings)	$560k
Reduce Warehouse Operating Expense	$15.5k
Reduce Obsolete Inventory (cost avoidance)	$400k

Figure 4.8   Case-in-Point Example 4.10 transformation results.

Case-in-Point Example 4.11 Anti-Lean Cost Savings

This case-in-point example reflects a company implementing a cost-savings initiative without considering the downstream repercussions. The company had an active continuous improvement program and strongly encouraged its staff to be innovative and identify cost savings opportunities.

This was a medical device manufacturer that had core processes where electronic circuitry was created for a blood-testing/-detection device by applying layers of a variety of conductive and detecting solutions.

The value stream leadership team within this solution-mixing and -application area brainstormed potential cost savings opportunities. One of the cost-savings initiatives was to increase the size (volume) of the solution-dispensing syringes. The benefits were two-fold:

■ There was always a small amount of solution retained in the smaller syringes that would be discarded. The larger syringes also retained a small amount of solution that needed to be discarded, but the accumulated amount discarded from ten small syringes exceeded the amount discarded from the one larger syringe.

■ It was less expensive to mix these solutions in one large batch rather than in ten small batches; the initial "small" syringes' volume was sized to process one lot of devices, while the new "large" syringes' volume would accommodate ten lots.

The various solutions were applied through a series of progressive automated solution dispensing and application equipment (only loading and unloading of the "lots" was manual). The "lots" typically went through five separate pieces of equipment in succession. The processing batches had to remain at ten lots of devices through all five types of processing equipment, so the lots had to wait for the completion of all one-lots before proceeding.

The simple diagram in Figure 4.9 shows the before and after scenarios.

This cost-savings initiative resulted in about $30k in annualized savings for all affected devices and was well received by the company's top management team.

But the $30k savings in solution usage (95%) and equipment set-ups (5%) came at the cost of a great creation of waste.

Waste was created through:

■ Inventory: Additional inventory (10x WIP at ~5 machines equaling 45 additional lots of devices, which is approximately an extra 450 minutes of process lead time);

■ Waiting: Equipment was shared among many devices, so to ensure proper control and proper set-up of the machine, no "lot" (batch) could be moved until all ten lots had been processed at each piece

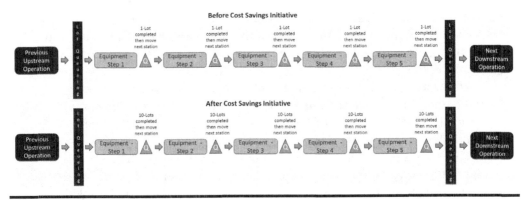

Figure 4.9 Before and after cost savings lot size impact.

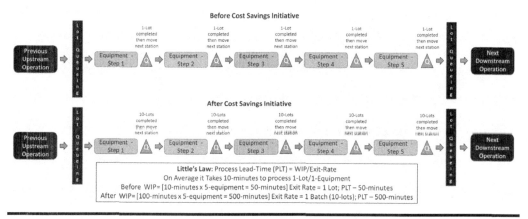

Figure 4.10   Before and after cost savings PLT impact.

equipment. These ten lots were all the same device type; thus, other device-types must queue if a lot (batch of 10) was being processed. This created additional overall waiting time and inventory (WIP). There were about 50 different types of devices that shared various pieces of equipment in the solution-dispensing area (maybe sharing one of the five types of equipment in this scenario, or maybe sharing all five; equipment and processes vary by device type, creating unevenness (mura));

- Overproduction: Ten lots vs. one lot;
- Mura: Unevenness as the flow was disrupted by large batch sizes of devices. Unevenness is mostly felt at the downstream operations, as they're expecting one lot at a time;
- Muri: The production system was designed and set up to run one lot at a time, so ten lots overburdens the production system's design (Figure 4.10).

The bottom line is that a $30k (~95% material scrap savings) cost savings resulted in larger amounts of inventory, additional planning/scheduling activities, and ad-hoc bottlenecks.

The lesson to be learned from this case story is the importance of having upstream and downstream stakeholders involved (or at least fully aware) in any initiative that might alter a process, material, documentation, etc.

I can recall a more serious situation in which a minor adjustment in a temperature setting to save a small amount of electrical usage resulted in a major customer recall of a medical device, probably costing the company millions of dollars. So be safe (reduce risks) and involve all stakeholders in project and/or decision making.

Index

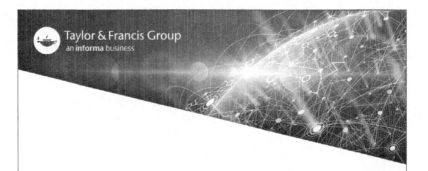